FOREWORD BY
**PATRICIA
RAYBON**

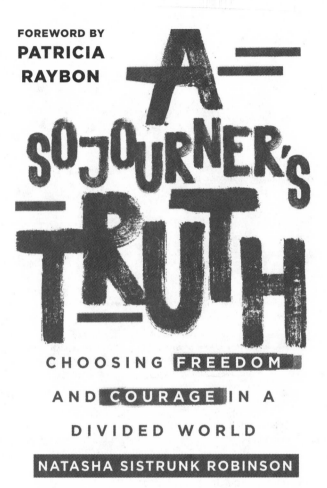

CHOOSING FREEDOM

AND COURAGE IN A

DIVIDED WORLD

NATASHA SISTRUNK ROBINSON

IVP Books

An imprint of InterVarsity Press
Downers Grove, Illinois

InterVarsity Press
P.O. Box 1400, Downers Grove, IL 60515-1426
ivpress.com
email@ivpress.com

InterVarsity Press® is the book-publishing division of InterVarsity Christian Fellowship/USA®, a movement of students and faculty active on campus at hundreds of universities, colleges, and schools of nursing in the United States of America, and a member movement of the International Fellowship of Evangelical Students. For information about local and regional activities, visit intervarsity.org.

All Scripture quotations, unless otherwise indicated, are taken from The Holy Bible, New International Version®, NIV®. Copyright © 1973, 1978, 1984, 2011 by Biblica, Inc.™ Used by permission of Zondervan. All rights reserved worldwide. www.zondervan.com. The "NIV" and "New International Version" are trademarks registered in the United States Patent and Trademark Office by Biblica, Inc.™

While any stories in this book are true, some names and identifying information may have been changed to protect the privacy of individuals.

Published in association with the literary agency of Credo Communications, LLC, Grand Rapids, MI, www.credocommunications.net.

Cover design: David Fassett
Interior design: Daniel van Loon
Images: ©IgorKrapar / iStock / Getty Images Plus

ISBN 978-0-8308-4552-1 (print)
ISBN 978-0-8308-7376-0 (digital)

Printed in the United States of America ∞

InterVarsity Press is committed to ecological stewardship and to the conservation of natural resources in all our operations. This book was printed using sustainably sourced paper.

Library of Congress Cataloging-in-Publication Data
A catalog record for this book is available from the Library of Congress.

P	21	20	19	18	17	16	15	14	13	12	11	10	9	8	7	6	5	4	3	2	1
Y	36	35	34	33	32	31	30	29	28	27	26	25	24	23	22	21	20	19	18		

"I love the way this woma
social relevance, Natash;
journey that empowers u
promised land of purpo
ommend this book!"

Brenda Salter McNeil, author of *A Credible Wit*

"Raw, vulnerable, and bold, Natasha Robin
honesty, courageous confession, and loving
this beautiful and poetic call to restoration,

Tara Beth Leach, senior pastor of PazNaz, author of *Emboldened*

"*A Sojourner's Truth* is a strikingly vulnerable work. In these pages, Natasha Sistrunk Robinson gifts us with her compelling story in hopes of setting us on a liberating path toward personal change, dependency on God, and faithful action. This book is right on time because it is capable of guiding women and men to genuine self-examination, growth, and leadership. We need Natasha's voice right now!"

Drew G. I. Hart, assistant professor of theology at Messiah College, author of *Trouble I've Seen*

"This book is a bridge over troubled waters and at times steps into those waters to reveal transformative truths about our broken world. Allow the powerful, troubling, reconciling, and dynamic words from Robinson to move you toward a life of deeper insight and impact."

Efrem Smith, copastor of Bayside Church Midtown, author of *Killing Us Softly*

"This message is right on time—and it couldn't come from a more trustworthy source! Natasha offers an innovative and liberating pathway to spiritual formation that will support all who seek to engage our divided world. Whether you are new to conversations around difference, division, and inequality, or a seasoned sojourner laboring under the weight of our divided world, Natasha's prophetic wisdom can guide you toward elevated and sustainable action."

Christena Cleveland, associate professor of the practice of organizational studies at Duke Divinity School, author of *Disunity in Christ*

"Natasha Robinson has lived it, experienced it, learned from it, and now through her writing, teaches us. The church needs truth telling. We are lost without the truth exposing secrets, lies, and false narratives. Natasha Robinson writes the truth that emerges from her own powerful narrative. She expresses the courage to speak the truth and to raise her voice. This is a voice the church needs to hear."

Soong-Chan Rah, Milton B. Engebretson Professor of Church Growth and Evangelism at North Park Theological Seminary, author of *The Next Evangelicalism* and *Prophetic Lament*

"Bold. Honest. Provocative. Wise. Natasha Robinson's voice brings all of these qualities to bear at a time when gracious but uncompromising truth telling is needed more than ever. Her personal story and biblical teaching connect us to God's heart on matters of compassion, justice, and leadership. She's the ideal guide for this tough but inspiring journey."

Edward Gilbreath, author of *Reconciliation Blues* and *Birmingham Revolution*

"This important, inspiring, and well-written book allows the light of truth to shine through uplifting—and at times heart-wrenching—stories and insights that use the theme of exodus as a guiding image. This book will stay with me for a long time."

James Bryan Smith, author of *The Good and Beautiful God*

"In *A Sojourner's Truth*, Natasha leads us through the story of Moses and through the raw reality of her own journey. Then Natasha leads us further still: she invites us to engage with our own story and our purpose in the world. Her exposition is profound, her cultural analysis is incisive and truth telling, and her personal story is both searing and vulnerable. This book is a must-read but also a must learn from!"

Jo Saxton, author of *More Than Enchanting*, cohost of the *Lead Stories* podcast

"Wrapping super-helpful teaching around a super-intriguing story, Natasha Sistrunk Robinson—in her prophetic voice—calls each of us toward greater self-insight, healing, and reconciliation. Natasha writes as she lives—with integrity of character—and shares inspirational stories of courage and devotion along with an always-present authenticity. Be prepared to be challenged!"

Debra Hirsch, missional leader and speaker, author of *Untamed* and *Redeeming Sex*

"With a swift and truthful pen, Natasha calls the reader to examine their personal history while she excavates American history and the biblical narrative. As a leader, mentor, and prophetic voice of justice, Natasha has written a work that is a guidebook and a guidepost, pushing the reader toward courage, boldness, and hope."

Amena Brown, spoken-word poet, author of *How to Fix a Broken Record*

"I am grateful for this sister's journey and for her willingness to share it. I am also grateful for her hard-won truth and her courage in declaring it. Read it and find clarity and courage to 'act, change, live, and stay on the redemptive path!'"

Ruth Haley Barton, founder of the Transforming Center, author of *Strengthening the Soul of Your Leadership*

"*A Sojourner's Truth* is Natasha Sistrunk Robinson's love letter to a stream of Christian faith familiar with compassion yet less familiar with justice. Through personal stories, keen biblical reflection, and straight talk about public policy, Natasha invites readers to rethink Christian discipleship. Revealing more and more of the truth of Jesus with each chapter, she leads readers on a sojourn well worth the taking."

Lisa Sharon Harper, founder and president of Freedom Road

FOR THE FOUNDERS:

Arthur Johnson, Jr.

Davede Alexander

QuaWanna Bannarbie

Tasya Lacy

Tracey Nicole Hayes

Thank you for catching the vision.

AND TO OUR LINKS LEADERS EVERYWHERE,

"Be strong and very courageous!"

IN MEMORIAM

Our son, Elijah Cortez Robinson

March 5, 2006

CONTENTS

FOREWORD

PATRICIA RAYBON

Natasha Sistrunk Robinson and I first met in the most prosaic of places—on Facebook. Everyone knows how tentative those initial interactions can sometimes be, but Natasha stood out. She was strong, clear-eyed, confident, a US Naval Academy graduate, a seminary graduate, and a former US Marine Corps officer. Watching her in even that pedestrian setting, I was left with one deep appeal: to truly know her. Or, as I asked when we finally were blessed to meet by video conference: *Tell me your story.* The real one. The brave one.

People of faith ask that of each other because we know there's always more than what is seen. Our surface is precisely that—our veneer. Under our Bible-studying, prayer-lifting, exegetical facades, we know our real truth awaits. People of color know this even more; our stories go untold. Looking to explain, we struggle to express our vexation—leaning on beloved warriors like Zora Neale Hurston, who wrote, "There's no agony like bearing an untold story inside you." Her words can feel mocked, however, when we learn they're often wrongly attributed—frequently to Dr. Maya Angelou, who is often misattributed herself. The mix-up affirms how, as people of color, our stories get wrongly shared, our personal details get lost, our worth gets minimized, and our courage gets undervalued (if it's ever even weighed).

Yet we soldier on, as African American theologian James H. Cone did, "in a society and in an intellectual discourse that did not even acknowledge that I existed." Letting our hair down all the way, however, exposes us to the bone, leaving us to declare with Audre Lorde, "If I didn't define myself for myself, I would be crunched into other people's fantasies for me and eaten alive."

In this book, you'll find a Cone-style, Lorde-blessed version of the warrior Natasha Sistrunk Robinson. Telling her own truth, she opens a vein. Telling all, she dares to help save herself, but also to galvanize the rest of us—maybe even to redeem us. From what? "That there is no place of safety for black people in America." Indeed, that "the American church is oftentimes too slow and too passive about almost everything that matters." Churched folks act, therefore, as if this rotten trouble were not a stench in God's nostrils or God couldn't strengthen us to help fight systemic injustice and fix it.

Well, God can.

In saying that, *A Sojourner's Truth* is an important book indeed. It is Natasha's story, but told on Natasha's terms. As she writes in her opening pages, "I am an expert on being me: a black, Christian woman from the South. So that's the story I'm telling."

I thought I knew "Tasha" well, but I needed to hear her hardest stories—that she struggled in vain to protect her light-skinned baby sister in a color-struck world. Or that her successful matriculation through military gauntlets brought her, literally, to her knees. With candor, she shares the pain and peculiarity of her family's "Negro poverty"—a wealth gap she deplores. As Natasha confesses, "My nasty, dirty little family secret is that we were poor."

With rich humility, Natasha unburies these raw family pearls— also granting equal time to the story of biblical Moses and the exodus plot of his own beleaguered people. As companion narratives, this material provides urgent, theological, "Sunday go to meeting" teaching. Natasha holds our reluctant feet to the fire.

This warrior is on a mission, indeed. For every ugly racial inequality still staining American soil and souls, she issues a battle cry to action, holding the body of Christ "accountable to Christ's standards, and to work together to become a loving, united, and righteous people of God."

In this brave volume, she invites us to kneel a while with her narrative and, as the saints of old used to say, to tarry there. Near her feet, humbled to look up and see God, we'll be inspired to do the right thing: to climb up from the mud and finally march.

PREFACE

There is power in bringing untold stories to light.
The freedom to speak about the reality of suffering
and death results in a freedom from denial.

RICHARD A. HORSLEY

Telling the truth can get you into trouble. I hear that in polite company we are not supposed to talk about religion, race, politics, or money. Now I'm here writing about all of them, although I am not an expert on any one. I am an expert on being me: a black, Christian woman from the South. So that's the story I'm telling. This is me using my power and writing my way to freedom.

Freedom. That's what I want for myself and for others now. It will come only when we tell the truth about ourselves, our environment, and the lives that we lead. The truth beckons us to stare reality in the face, to embrace the scars of our suffering, and to confess when death and the shadows of death change our lives forever. If we want freedom, then the truth cannot be denied.

The truth is, my faith, skin color, gender, and culture have significantly informed the ways God calls me to respond, speak, and act in this world. I am human. I've suffered quite a bit of loss and have wrestled with the tensions and intersectionality of being both black and woman (more on that later).

I am deeply convicted by the darkness of this world, and I am calling people to walk in the light. This book reveals two convictions in particular.

First, *we need to hear more stories that originate with and feature the voices and experiences of people of color.* We don't need folks telling us about people of color. We all benefit when people of color clearly, directly, and authentically use their own words, research, history, work, and art to courageously tell about their whole lives and present their whole selves if they so choose.

Second, *we need to see more women and men working and leading together across generations to advance the kingdom of God.* If this is to happen, then more women must recognize and take ownership of their responsibilities to lead, regardless of how or where they work and in spite of whether or not they have a title or formal position. Likewise, we need more men, particularly those in positions of power, educating themselves out of their own ignorance, leading the fight against injustices to women and people of color, and creating leadership opportunities, mentorship, and sponsorship for women and ethnic minorities.

Because of these convictions, I have rendered my heart and committed these words to paper. I am inviting you to experience the presence and wisdom of God with me. I trust that he will speak to you as you are guided through my story.

I also invite you to a historical transport through the story of Moses and the exodus. This biblical narrative has had great significance for generations of African American Christians because of its message of liberation. From slavery to the civil rights movement to now, this story offers truth and hope for all who feel unknown, unloved, uncertain, out of sorts, or misunderstood for any number of reasons. I know that the transatlantic slave trade was not the same as the enslavement of the Israelites, that ancient Egypt is not modern-day America, and that African Americans are not the same as God's chosen people, Israel. However, all Christians are God's elect, and that means this exodus narrative is a part of our shared history. We can read, learn, and study it for its own sake and also for ours (see 1 Corinthians 10). This book provides a unique opportunity for you to explore the Scriptures from the vantage point of someone who, like Moses, was born into a marginalized people group.

Along the way I will offer quite a bit of social and cultural commentary. Growing up I remember the old folks saying, "Don't be so heavenly minded that you're no earthly good." God cares about this world, and he desires for his kingdom to come on earth as it is in heaven. As sojourners, we understand that the earth as we now know it is only our temporary home. However, as kingdom citizens—those given the authority to work and make God's kingdom known now—we must survey our social, political, and cultural climates to discern how God wants us to courageously speak and respond to the current issues of our day.

But before we can respond to God's call to follow in our modern day, we must address soul-defining questions such as:

Who or what is worthy of my worship?

For what purpose has God created me?

What stories or life experiences is God using to shape me?

How will I choose freedom and courage as I faithfully live out my purpose or calling?

The first person each of us must learn to speak truth to is ourselves. The first person we must learn to lead is ourselves. So this is me, inviting you to answer the questions, to speak the truth, to lead well, and to become strong and courageous.

PART ONE

FORMATION

In the beginning God created the heavens and the earth.

GENESIS 1:1

Beginnings have meaning. Beginnings reveal the purpose and value of our lives by shaping us into the people we are to become.

Likewise, the purpose of our lives is often revealed through the teaching, examples, experiences, messages, and disappointments we encounter in our formative years. These shaping elements determine how we grow and respond in the world. Over time God takes the good messages and refines them. If we allow him, he also takes the bad messages—the uncertainties, the lies, and the unbelief—and replaces them with truth.

In sharing my truth, I'm giving you the opportunity to eavesdrop on the internal wrestling of my heart, and I'm also taking you on a biblical expedition to journey with Moses. Here we make a sojourn through his birth to his calling, where he comes face-to-face with God and finds his life's purpose.

God reveals the truth about himself to Moses in this dramatic encounter. Can you imagine how difficult it is to trust this God in a culture of many gods, and to still hold on to hope when you can see only glimmers of his promises at best? Learning to trust God— whether enslaved or free, well fed or hungry, in times of war and in times of peace, dwelling in the palace, the wilderness, or the promised land filled with giants—is the spiritual act of knowing and then obeying the truth.

CHAPTER ONE

TRUTH IS, YOUR IDENTITY CAN
GET YOU INTO HOT WATER

If you are silent about your pain, they'll
kill you and say you enjoyed it.

ZORA NEALE HURSTON

*I*t was a forbidden conversation.

"Carmen, Momma says I have to always be there for you," I told my younger sister. "Some white people are not going to like you because you are black, and some black people are not going to like you because you are light skinned."

I had waited a long time before sharing this information that my mother had relayed to me in secret. I was only a child, in middle or early high school. I didn't really understand the significance of these words, and I don't know how I expected my little sister to respond when I told her this truth. But I was surprised and even shocked to see tears well up in her eyes, fall down to her cheeks, and land in the palms of her hands as she began to gasp for breath and cry uncontrollably.

"What's wrong?" I asked, confused and uncertain now.

As she tried to control her body, she looked up at me and said, "People don't like me."

I didn't know what to do with that response.

It wasn't until many years later that I became aware of the brown paper bag tests. Author and professor Michael Eric Dyson wrote, "In fact, New Orleans invented the brown paper bag party—usually at a gathering in a home—where anyone darker than the bag attached to the door was denied entrance. The brown bag criterion survives as a metaphor for how the black cultural elite quite literally establishes a caste system along color lines within black life." For black people in general, it's the epitome of self-hate brought on by the reality that we are not white in a society that normalizes all things white as pure, right, and better. For the black elite, the test was a way to maintain the pride, self-righteous assurance, and soothing comfort of knowing that they were not poor. There was no need for social mingling with black people who were dark skinned or impoverished, because those people were not marriage material.

Thank God my sister and I had a loving mother—a black woman who would not set her black daughters up for failure. As we grew, she told us the truth about the hardships we would likely face in this world, and she didn't hold back. My mother warned us about the setup of systemic racism and cultural biases (although she did not use those terms), and she had a hope for a better future for us all.

So there I was, sitting next to my younger sister trying to have an adult-like conversation. At the time my sister's lighter skin color would have passed the brown paper bag test, and my browner complexion would not.

In that moment, the message "People don't like you" is not what I wanted to communicate at all. I saw my sister's tears and thought, *What on earth have I done?* What I wanted her to hear was, "My sista, don't you worry about a thing because no matter what happens in this world and who stands against you, I have your back. You can trust that, and you can trust me."

There is truth in the statement "When one person hurts in a family, everyone aches. And this is always the choice: pain demands to be felt—or it will demand you feel nothing as all." My sister was born a light-skinned black woman in America, and this would be the source of her pain. To some extent, I suppose this was the source of my pain as well. Along with that pain, I felt my first yearning of leadership in my longing to protect my vulnerable little sister. Yet I couldn't even safeguard myself. And I was powerless to defend her.

This was the moment I realized that things were not quite right in this world.

LIFE OF THE BROKEN AND BROKENHEARTED

Miriam's story resonated with me because she too was charged with watching her younger sibling. We meet Miriam at the beginning of the book of Exodus keeping a vigilant eye over her baby brother, Moses, as he drifts down the Nile River. Miriam was a servant and faithful witness, but she seems to appear only as a footnote in the story. At first glance, we all think this story is about baby Moses. But the story is actually bigger than Moses, and it's bigger than Miriam. To better understand Moses' journey, we have to start at the beginning because what happens in our formative years has a way of shaping our adult lives. As we reflect, we come to understand that Moses' story and ours are all a part of God's redemptive story.

God's big story of creation, fall, and redemption is steeped in pain. For godly people and leaders specifically, pain is often the tool God uses to help us realize our passion and purpose. Being exposed to the reality of racism as a child and feeling helpless to do anything about it revealed my pain. For Moses, the pain was revealed in the basket that held his three-month-old body afloat in the water. It was not a pain that he bore—not yet anyway—but it was the pain of his community.

He was in the basket because the king of Egypt, consumed by his own fears and desire for population control, issued a death sentence on all newborn Hebrew boys. The pain of death—the reality that this boy would surely die if he remained at home with his biological family—is what put baby Moses in the basket. The pain of his mother, Jochebed, and her last hope to save his life is what put him in the basket. The pain of the heavy hand of an oppressor and more than four hundred years of his people's enslavement is what put Moses in the basket. The pain of the possibility that God

> Pain is often the tool God uses to help us realize our passion and purpose.

had forgotten them is what put him in that basket. As a baby he could not carry that pain, but this pain landed him in the basket, floating down the Nile.

In reading we learn quickly that the Exodus narrative is not just a story about Moses or his sister, Miriam. Exodus teaches us about what God is doing in the midst of a people group to accomplish his will on earth. God had heard the cries of the enslaved Hebrew community, and he intended to do something about it.

God would use Moses to deliver his people out of their pain.

From the time captured Africans were bought to America and enslaved, they have longed for deliverance. But more than deliverance, they longed for the freedom to speak their own names, to preserve their own history, to keep their own property, to protect their own families, to work and enjoy the fruits of their own labor, to govern themselves, to tell their own stories, and perhaps to get some relief from their painful reality. Humanity is lost when slavery is normalized.

As a child, I didn't understand the biblical history, the mysteries of God, or his plan for my life. However, I did know when something hurt. I sat with my pain as I watched my sister in silence, and perhaps for the first time in my life I began to experience the pain of the entire black community. I was heartbroken and remained at her side until I thought she would be okay, but our pain did not go away. In the same manner, Miriam "stood at a distance to see what would happen" to her baby brother, because she had no real control over or assurance of his safety (Exodus 2:4).

Acknowledging our pain makes us vulnerable.

VULNERABILITY AND SILENCE

Vulnerability can be dangerous in the same way water is dangerous. Like water, vulnerability can be the source of cleansing and renewal or it can be the source of drowning and death. But there is something else that is more dangerous than taking the risk of vulnerability, and that is silence.

As an African American woman who loves my African American sistas, I have learned that we are often silent about what hurts us the most. Dr. Chanequa Walker-Barnes refers to this epidemic as a "Deadly Silence." She writes:

> Perhaps nowhere in society is the StrongBlackWoman more ubiquitous than in the Christian church. The church reinforces the mythology of the StrongBlackWoman by silencing, ignoring, and even romanticizing the suffering of Black women. Rather than offering a balm to heal the wounds of Black women who cry out about their pain, the church admonishes them with platitudes such as "God won't give you any more than you can bear" and "If He brought you to it, He'll bring you through it."

Acclaimed Harlem Renaissance writer Zora Neale Hurston was also a black woman acquainted with suffering, and she understood that we, as African Americans, could not be silent about our pain because silence would be the death of us. By swallowing the poison of our pain, we die a slow death, and for black people in America it seems as if nobody notices. As another artist wrote, "The heart dies a slow death, shedding each hope like leaves until one day there are none. No hopes. Nothing remains."

Knowing the pain, history, violence, and silence that have shaped the African American narrative infuses how I read the Scriptures. I come from a marginalized and oppressed people group that was enslaved for more than three hundred years, so I try to imagine the helplessness and hopelessness that the Hebrew people felt as an entire generation of their boys were thrown into the Nile River. What would be worse: knowing that the actual genocide took place, knowing that people in positions of power in the empire stood by and said nothing, or knowing that nothing would be done about this loss of innocent lives—that justice would not be served? This is a painful narrative that is quite familiar to African Americans. Murder by the state. Silence. Then nothing. The heart dies a slow death. The painful reality of this death emotionally cripples us, and black people have been conditioned to say, "Thank you," and take our lethal doses with a smile.

If healing is to come, then this pain must be named and confronted.

But I am not without hope. We see from Moses' story that God hears the cries of the oppressed. God enters our pain, through our suffering, even in the silence. If healing is to come, then this pain must be named and confronted. We cannot look away. With every truth-telling moment, we can better discern what these moments reveal about our history, our authentic selves, our leadership journey, and our hope for a better future. Only then can we challenge each other to join in God's great work of justice, redemption, and reconciliation.

LET THIS ENCOUNTER WITH WATER CHANGE YOU

The power and wealth of the Egyptians prevented them from considering the pain that slavery inflicted on the Hebrew people. All the while, the Hebrews were crying out to God for their deliverance. Neither the Egyptians nor the Hebrews knew that one infant's trip to the water—a trip that could have meant life or death for him—would turn the tide and usher in freedom for an entire people group. This divine hope was made possible through the most unlikely source—the compassion of Pharaoh's daughter. When she discovered Moses floating in the water, she made a choice to see a human, not just a Hebrew boy.

Like Pharaoh's daughter, our healing from a sin-sick, power-driven, money-hungry, and racialized culture will come only when we learn to see differently. None of us really knows how one empathetic gesture, one listening ear, one kind word spoken, or one loving act can change the trajectory of a person's life. With her actions, Pharaoh's daughter made it possible for Moses to grow into manhood, in which he eventually learned that God always sets before us choices of life or death, blessings or curses. As Moses later instructed the Israelites:

> This day I call the heavens and the earth as witnesses against you that I have set before you life and death, blessings and curses. Now choose life, so that you and your children may live and that you may love the LORD your God, listen to his voice, and hold fast to him. (Deuteronomy 30:19-20)

Pharaoh's daughter reminds us that with every word and act, we choose either life or death for ourselves and for others.

Just as the physical act of Moses' mother placing him into the water and the physical act of Pharaoh's daughter drawing him out of it express their choices, our physical actions reveal the internal condition of our souls and whether or not we are truly responding to God. Choosing life means participating in God's redemptive work as he transforms families, reshapes communities, and converts nations. Whenever we do the hard or courageous thing in spite of our lack of understanding, our familial upbringing, our own pain, or difficult circumstances, we are choosing life.

AN INVITATION FOR THE VULNERABLE

As the old spiritual says,

> Take me to the water,
> take me to the water,
> take me to the water
> to be baptized.
>
> Nothing but the righteous,
> nothing but the righteous,
> nothing but the righteous
> shall see God.

We want to see God—to be aware of his presence—but so often we miss him because we are evaluating the wrong things in the wrong way. We try to determine whether God is at work based on our own prosperity and temporal "blessings." However, the Bible has a different standard of evaluation. Through Moses' story we learn that God communes with us in the mountaintop experiences of our lives, but also in the wilderness, on the long walk to freedom, and in the waves of the wild and dangerous waters.

God is with me in the water—to rescue me from all the consuming patterns of thought that remain from a life and history of being enslaved. Let there be no doubt that we have all been enslaved to something. Like Pharaoh and his daughter, Jochebed and her husband, Moses and his sister, we all have different encounters with and proximity to the water. Our interaction with the water allows us to consider whether we will aim to command it or allow it to transform us.

We can come thirsty, helpless, and weak, acknowledging our desperate need for change. That is when God meets and rescues us.

Get baptized and come out anew. Go into or come out of the troubled waters. That's the invitation from God to each of us. Enter into the pain and suffering of this life to find your purpose and passion through a new life. Because we have been conditioned to swallow or ignore the ever-present sin and pain, we need a spiritual baptism into a new way of thinking, being, and responding in this world. Jesus' invitation is "Come to me, all you who are weary and burdened, and I will give you rest. . . . For I am gentle and humble in heart, and you will find rest for your souls" (Matthew 11:28-29). We have an invitation to lay our pain and burdens down.

When teaching about leadership and follower-ship, Jesus also said, "Truly I tell you, unless you change and become like little children, you will never enter the kingdom of heaven. Therefore, whoever takes the lowly position of this child is the greatest in the kingdom of heaven" (Matthew 18:3-4). We must come like that three-month-old baby 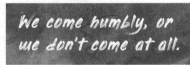 boy floating in the river or like the little children who came to Jesus—realizing that there is nothing on earth we can do for ourselves. We come humbly, or we don't come at all.

Death awaits us if we stay in hiding or if we float adrift in the water, and if we want to live, we desperately need someone to come and lift us up out of it. We come with our pain, which eventually connects us to our purpose and passion, and then leads us into praise.

THE MYSTERY OF PAIN AND WEAKNESS

I've got so much to thank God for.
So many wonderful blessings and so many open doors.
A brand-new mercy, along with each new day.
That's why I praise you.

We stood in front of many congregations as our soloist sang these opening words from Kurt Carr's song "For Every Mountain." I planted my feet and stood proudly in my service dress blue uniform as a member of the United States Naval Academy Gospel Choir. Many of us were African American and first-generation college students, and life was hard. As we listened and then sang, we remembered our various trials: studying in the wee hours of the night, those who had left us and would not graduate, and those who we left still struggling back home. I remembered all of the failed swim tests before I eventually passed and could graduate. I remembered my pain, and I sang praises to the Lord. That singing sometimes turned into tears, or raised hands, or shouts of "Hallelujah," or praise dancing. While God does not always remove our pain and suffering, he does not abandon us in the troubled waters of life. He is present to carry us up, over, or through.

The apostle Paul was honest about his struggles. He asked God to take them away, but God did not. In fact, God's word of comfort to Paul was simply this: "My grace is sufficient for you, for my power is made perfect in weakness." God promised to be *enough* for Paul, so Paul's response was praise: "Therefore I will boast all the more gladly about my weaknesses, so that Christ's power may rest on me. That is why, for Christ's sake, I delight in weaknesses, in insults, in hardships, in persecutions, in difficulties. For when I am weak, then I am strong" (2 Corinthians 12:9-10).

Can we get real with ourselves and each other for a moment? None of this makes any sense. Weaknesses, insults, hardships, persecution, and difficulties cause us deep pain and suffering. Yet it is often in our pain and in our torment that we experience God's grace, and the painful experiences strengthen and refine us. This is what some scholars and theologians refer to as the upside-down kingdom of God: what makes sense, looks right, or feels good to us is often not the Lord's way.

This is why Jesus teaches that if someone slaps our right cheek, we should offer them up the left one to slap as well (Matthew 5:39). I'm not sanctified enough to offer up my face like that! Let's be clear: Jesus is not promoting violence or domestic abuse, but he is teaching about our responsibilities as peacemakers. We are not to respond or to treat other people as their sins deserve. We must not seek our own revenge.

There are rewards for this peacemaking behavior because the bigger objective of Jesus' teaching is to reveal the purposes of his kingdom. In his kingdom, the first will be last and the last will be first (Matthew 20:1-16). In his kingdom, redeemed slaves and their former masters, the poor and the rich, the powerless and the powerful, will sit at the table together. In his kingdom, you can go into the water dirty and come out of it clean. Jesus promises to use the foolish things of this world to confound the wise, and "the weak things of the world to shame the strong" (1 Corinthians 1:26-27). If we are going to make it in this upside-down life, we need to see God's grace at work in our pain and in our weaknesses.

God's power can be revealed through us if we simply get out of thinking that we know more than we actually do, or that we can effectively respond beyond our sinful human limitations without accepting this invitation from Christ. God invites us to confess our pain. Come as little children. Depend on him. Praise him for our weaknesses, Paul says! Not only that, but we are also to delight in our insults, in our hardships, in our persecutions, and in our difficulties. And these painful life experiences are to lead us into praise? Help us, oh Lord!

In our weaknesses, God's grace is revealed. God's grace is revealed when people like my mother tell the truth about life, and when people like Moses' mother or Pharaoh's daughter take risks to preserve a child's life. Because we are vulnerable humans, we all need somebody to have our backs, to tell the truth, to take risks, to safeguard us, to lift us up out of the water, and to show us a better way. Paul's mysterious boasting and praise reveals that Jesus has done this for us. Because of Jesus, God can use our pain to inform us so we can all be better together—even with our diverse backgrounds.

Through our pain and in our weaknesses, we are collectively made strong.

TRUTH IS: We all suffer from pain, and God uses that pain to shape us for his good kingdom purposes.

REFLECTION QUESTION: Ann Voskamp writes, "Not one thing in your life is more important than figuring out how to live in the face of unspoken pain." What is the source of your pain?

SCRIPTURE MEDITATION: "The LORD is close to the brokenhearted and saves those who are crushed in spirit" (Psalm 34:18).

PERSONAL AFFIRMATION: I can trust God with my pain, understanding that pain can serve as a catalyst to finding my passion and purpose.

CALL TO ACTION: We start with our own healing. Are there any steps you need to take to process pain that has surfaced for you?

PRAYER: God, I thank you that you have not abandoned me in my weakness. You have not left me alone in this world to fight for myself. You are ever present, ever caring, and ever loving to take me through my pain. Help me to trust you to do this sacred work. In the power and authority of your son, Jesus', name. Amen.

TWEET: We come with our pain, which eventually connects us to our purpose and passion, and then leads us into praise. @asistasjourney #ASojournersTruth

CHAPTER TWO

TRUTH IS, WOMEN ARE THE UNSUNG HEROES IN THIS WORLD

Where did your Christ come from? From God and a woman! Man had nothing to do with him!

SOJOURNER TRUTH, "AIN'T I A WOMAN?"

She gently touched my shoulder, then took my hand to lift me from the brown folding chair under the funeral-home tent. My eyes had been fixed on the steel silver bars as I watched strangers lower my mother's body into the ground. My Aunt Janet said to me, "Come on inside the church, Tasha. There are some things you just don't need to see."

I don't remember eating the meal provided at the church that day. I don't remember what I did before or after the service. I don't remember whether I wore my midshipman service dress blue uniform or a traditional black dress—it wasn't exactly a day for taking pictures. I do remember entering the old Baptist church, filled with family and friends, as songs of praise rang out from a full choir loft where my mother used to sing. Those black people, my mother's friends, stomped, rocked, and clapped their hands as they sang praises to Jesus. As I walked down the aisle, I worried about my immediate family: How would we make it without my mother? Who would love and lead us now?

My high school principal was one of the officials who carried the ceremonial flowers to the small gravesite outside, and she was allowed to sit in the front of the church until it was time to perform her duty. She called me several days later and said, "You know, Tasha, I watched you that whole service, and the only time you cried was when you looked at your immediate family. Somehow, you knew you were going to be alright because your mother gave you enough love to last a lifetime."

The truth was, I first experienced God's grace to me through the love and sacrifices of my dear mother.

The most difficult thing about her death was knowing that she would no longer share the important moments in my life. She would not be there to see me graduate from the United States Naval Academy. She would not be there to see me marry. She would not be present for the birth of my children—the son lost and the daughter who remains. My heart's deepest ache was not having an answer for the questions, *Who is going to love me like my momma? How do you define a home without her?*

I was sad and lonely. I poured myself into work. For years I bottled my emotions and did not sufficiently grieve. But when I thought I would emotionally die, God was gracious. He sustained my life by bringing other women who continued to show up when I needed motherly support.

When I returned to the Naval Academy and resumed college life, it was my mentor, Mary Thompson, who provided a haven for prayer, home-cooked meals, and a safe place for my many tears. When I graduated, it was my godmother, Mrs. Joyce Garrett, and her husband, Pop, who threw my best friend and me a graduation party because our lives, our accomplishments, and our new careers in the military were worth celebrating.

When I got married, it was my other godmother, Sister Linda Jones, who managed the wedding. I was not anxious because she was running the show. When my bridesmaids left my hotel room to head to the church, two of their mothers remained to help me get dressed and drive me to the church on that bright spring day. As my dear friends were preparing to stand as my witnesses, their mothers were taking care of me. I didn't ask them to do that; they just showed up. On that day there were no tears of sadness because I did not have my one and only mother. God in his grace had given me three.

One of Jesus' best friends, the apostle John, wrote of him, "From his fullness we have all received, grace upon grace" (John 1:16 NRSV). This truth I know full well.

A STRONG BLACK WOMAN

God's grace sustains us through our beginnings and endings. Losing my mom when I was twenty felt like the end of being a daughter and the beginning of being a mother to my younger siblings—my sister and brother. I grew up very quickly in the four and a half years between mom's funeral and my wedding. I became more responsible for myself—and for my father and siblings as well. There is a weightiness to becoming a matriarch. So, I learned to fully embrace that I am a strong woman and a leader.

I don't wear the "strong woman" title as a badge of honor, as if I had a blue leotard with a Superwoman emblem on my chest and a red cape flying in the wind—not anymore, anyway. I used to be the StrongBlackWoman that Chanequa Walker-Barnes describes:

[She] is the woman who constantly extends herself on behalf of others. In her intimate and family relationships, on her job, and in her church and community, she is the "go to" woman, the one upon whom others depend when they need assistance, counsel, or comfort. Driven by a deeply ingrained desire to be seen as helpful and caring, she is practically incapable of saying no to others' requests without experiencing feelings of guilt and worthlessness. As her willingness to help repeatedly reinforces others' tendencies to ask her for help, her very nature becomes defined by multitasking and over-commitment.

I still multitask, but I have learned to say no by establishing boundaries, setting aside the responsibilities that do not belong to me, and asking for help.

I have also learned that strong is not always the opposite of weak. Strong is knowing your own power and exercising it humbly. In his book *Strong and Weak*, Andy Crouch writes, "What we truly admire in human beings is not authority alone or vulnerability alone—we seek both together." Being a strong black woman is knowing quite deeply that the two—strength and weakness, authority and vulnerability—can coexist. This knowing is often born out of much suffering and sorrow.

> *Strong is knowing your own power and exercising it humbly.*

WHEN DEATH COMES KNOCKING

My mother's death was the third significant loss in my life. It was the beginning of a period of sixteen years in which I lost eleven close family members. For a long stretch of time, I only went home to attend funerals. It is hard to see a hopeful future when death is always knocking at your door. The temptation is to magnify all that you are losing, rather than focus on what remains for you to hold on to.

Ten years into this wilderness, my husband and I lost our first child. I carried him for five months—both he and I were healthy—

and then I unexpectedly miscarried. The day before his death, I bought his first outfits from Old Navy along with a cuddly teddy bear. We wanted our child to have a strong biblical name, so we named him Elijah after the prophet and after my maternal grandfather, who we had also lost.

On the morning of Elijah's death, I rose from bed like any other day. My husband and I were visiting our godparents at Camp Lejeune, North Carolina. We went to a restaurant for breakfast and were preparing to drive home, but something did not feel right. Without any pain at all, I sensed that the baby had dropped.

When we went to the emergency room, the nurse affirmed our deepest fear. I would deliver Elijah, and he was not going to make it. I took the drugs. They minimized the pain so it did not feel like I was having a real labor, and they caused me to sleep directly afterward. In my weakness and heartbreak, I could not even muster the strength to look at my stillborn son, but my godmother held him in her arms and bore witness to his presence in this world.

I took my weak and vulnerable self from that cold hospital room to the loving hospitability of my godmother's home and couch, where I remained for several days. God's grace to me was the safety and shelter of that home.

A dear friend came to the house after a long day's work to sit with me. After a lengthy silence, she said, "You know, it's okay to cry."

I lifted my head from the pillow, took my eyes off the *Meerkat Manor* show I had been binge watching all day, and informed her, "I'm all cried out. Been crying all day. Don't feel like crying right now. If you want to cry, go right ahead." But this Marine Corps officer, my sister, responded by holding back her tears. God's grace to me was that she came, she sat, she bore witness, and she loved me with her presence, her silence, and her hidden tears.

Then there was my friend Lisa, who lifted me from my bed to minister her old-school remedy of using cabbage to dry up my milk because my breasts hurt. She cracked jokes as she packed my bra full of cabbage, and I cried through that laughter. Only a few years later, some of these same women were in the room to hold my hands and feet and to cheer me on as I delivered our beautiful baby girl.

Life. New births. Funerals. Deaths. Disappointments. These are things that we don't have any control over. When life happens, the best we can do is show up for it and be fully present. This is a spiritual discipline that I have specifically learned from black women. We consistently show up to comfort, to sustain, to grieve, to celebrate, and to start something new. When times get hard and threaten to take us out, God in his magnificent grace provides people who will show up for us to make our tragic lives bearable.

I suspect that you have witnessed this grace at work in your own life. The many ways that we experience God's grace—both big and small—are common to all of us. As we grow in age and maturity, we realize that things aren't always as they should be, and our lives may not be as we had hoped. You see, strong women and leaders are not superhuman. We all have personal struggles.

It is in this reality that we come to better understand our true selves and our commonalities, and it is here that we come face-to-face with God. God's common grace is in the blessings of loving mothers (either biological, adopted, or self-appointed), aunts who show us how to hold on and when to let go, and friends who know how to laugh, cry, or sit in silence. We all need each other. Our human lives require interdependency. Having someone show up at the opportune time is a means of God's grace to us.

SAVED BY GRACE

Before Miriam showed up for her brother, the exodus story began with two women rescuers: the Hebrew midwives, Shiphrah and Puah. When Pharaoh gave the order for the midwives to kill all the Hebrew boys, they refused. They rejected the murderous plan of the empire because they feared God more than the king (Exodus 1:15-21). It was a significant risk to defy Pharaoh, and by doing so these women saved vulnerable lives while looking death, danger, and darkness in the face. That was the first time Moses' life was saved by women.

Next, Pharaoh ordered that all the Hebrew infant boys be thrown into the Nile, while the girls would be spared (Exodus 1:22). The Nile River was a symbol of life to the Egyptians, but it offered a grave reminder to the Hebrews that their boys had no right to live. This genocide plot caused Moses' mother to spring into action to save her son's life.

Then Pharaoh's daughter rescued Moses when she drew him out of the water. When she opened the basket, she noticed right away that it was a Hebrew baby—but she made no mention that he was a boy. Perhaps before Pharaoh's daughter even noticed the baby's gender, Miriam jumped in to ask, "Shall I go and get one of the Hebrew women to nurse the baby for you?"

> "Yes, go," she answered. So the girl went and got the baby's mother. Pharaoh's daughter said to her, "Take this baby and nurse him for me, and I will pay you." So the woman took the baby and nursed him. When the child grew older, she took him to Pharaoh's daughter and he became her son. She named him Moses, saying, "I drew him out of the water." (Exodus 2:7-10)

Among the enslaved Hebrew people and among many grieving mothers who had lost their sons, Jochebed got paid to do what she would have gladly done for free. So baby Moses' life was thrice saved from death: by the wisdom and courage of the midwives, by his mother's plan, and by Pharaoh's daughter's compassion.

Moses grew up, and more than forty years later he married a woman named Zipporah. Together they had a son named Gershom (Exodus 2:21-22). When Moses did not circumcise the child as

God had instructed Abraham as part of his covenant (see Genesis 17:10-14; 21:4), it was Zipporah who performed the righteous act that stopped the Lord from killing Moses. And again, his life was spared by a woman (Exodus 4:24-26).

It's plain to see that Moses became a rescuer because his life was rescued. Without the leadership and obedience of the women in his life, God's plan for him would have been aborted. God's grace was consistently revealed in Moses' life through the presence of wise, faithful, and risk-taking women.

When I think about my own life and how I have become a leader, it is impossible to separate my story from the women who have shaped me. Like Moses, my life has been saved by the sacrifices, contributions, and faithful obedience of women. But the strong female influences in my early life were not due to the absence of faithful black men in my community. There were simply more women in my biological family.

> God's grace was consistently revealed in Moses' life through the presence of wise, faithful, and risk-taking women.

By and large, women have been the agents of grace in my life, teaching me how to live, grow, stand tall, pray, take God at his Word, worship, praise, and, perhaps most importantly, laugh out loud. This is how women have consistently showed up to save my life, and I don't know where I would be without them.

And women are the unsung heroes of Moses' story. Men *and* women need to hear this message! We quickly forget that the Hebrew midwives refused to participate in the genocide, that Moses' mother initiated a strategic plan, that his sister stood watch, that Pharaoh's daughter hospitably welcomed him into her home in spite of his pedigree, and that his wife obeyed God when he did not. These women were leaders who served as God's grace and protection for Moses to ensure that he would rise as a leader among his people to fulfill the purpose God had for his life. God's saving grace to all of us is often revealed through the bosoms, the hands, the teaching, the correction, the unconditional love, the sacrifices, the laughter, the truth telling, and the risks of faithful women. We must not forget to regularly acknowledge their leadership and thank God for them.

TRUTH IS: God's grace is evident in our lives, and often it is the faithful witness, presence, and actions of women that remind us of this truth.

REFLECTION QUESTION: In what ways have women showed up to minister God's grace to you?

SCRIPTURE MEDITATION: "[God] said to me, 'My grace is sufficient for you, for my power is made perfect in weakness.' Therefore I will boast all the more gladly about my weaknesses, so that Christ's power may rest on me. That is why, for Christ's sake, I delight in weaknesses, in insults, in hardships, in persecutions, in difficulties. For when I am weak, then I am strong" (2 Corinthians 12:9-10).

PERSONAL AFFIRMATION: From the fullness of God's grace I have received one blessing after another (John 1:16).

CALL TO ACTION: Reach out to a woman who has ministered God's grace to you and thank her.

PRAYER: Dear God, your grace keeps me looking forward to tomorrow. Help me to trust and know that death is not the end of my story. You are the author and finisher of all things, and out of death and darkness you invite me to experience light and new life. For this, I thank you and give you praise. Amen.

TWEET: It is tempting to magnify all that you are losing, rather than focus on what remains for you to hold on to. @asistasjourney #ASojournersTruth

CHAPTER THREE

COMMUNITY

TRUTH IS, THERE IS NO
PLACE LIKE HOME

The Negro is the child of two cultures—Africa
and America. The problem is that in the search
for wholeness all too many Negros seek to
embrace only one side of their natures.

MARTIN LUTHER KING JR.

ong before I knew I was a Christian or a leader, I understood that I was black and a woman. When people ask me about myself, when they are trying to define or understand my identity, I begin with the simple statement, "I am a black girl from Orangeburg, South Carolina." This is the core of who I am. I was actually born in the state's capital of Columbia, but I was raised in Orangeburg. Being a child of that small town in the '80s and '90s shaped how I saw myself and particularly how I saw other black people. Black people were all around this town, which is home to two Historically Black Colleges and Universities (HBCUs): South Carolina State University and Claflin University. Orangeburg is where I learned and embodied black culture and experience.

This was my community—the place where I belonged, where I was affirmed, and where I was shaped into a leader. As Reggie McNeal wrote, "Leaders are not shaped in isolation. Leaders are shaped in community. And they are shaped by community. Leaders cannot be separated from the formative processes of community. Despite any claims to the contrary, leaders are not self-made people. There is no such person. God deliberately and intentionally shapes the leader's heart through community." My community is where I was shaped by the words of the Negro National Anthem "Lift Every Voice and Sing." The black people in my community sang proudly as all the generations, young and old, stumbled over the choppy chorus lyrics:

Sing a song full of the faith that the dark past has taught us,
Sing a song full of the hope that the present has brought us.

Then we raised our voices together, as a hopeful people purposed to triumph:

Facing the rising sun of our new day begun,
Let us march on 'til victory is won.

I was formed by the fortitude of my people. I come from a marching—and "march on until"—type of people. We have the marching, cosmic rhythm of the step team that reminds us of our stripped African heritage; this is quite different from the march of the dance, which often celebrates our freedom—the victories won and the victories yet to come. Then there is the celebration march of the band, particularly the South Carolina State University Marching 101 Band. It was their step, their high knee, their rhythm and blues, the blaring of their horns, the beauty and aggression of their dance, the beat and warring of their drums that allowed me to call this place home.

> I was formed by the fortitude of my people.

I watched and learned and reveled in it all because I was black. This black culture and my existence in this community shaped me during my formative years.

LES CHARMES CLUB

Community reflects culture, and culture is what a collective group does together to affirm their identity, history, and values. The vibrancy of the HBCU culture filtered through the cracks of the town's only public high school, Orangeburg Wilkinson High, where we also lived the college life (apart from the coursework and dormitories). The desire to mimic the college experience led to my pledging as a high school freshman and later becoming president of the sorority Les Charmes Club (LCC). Our motto was "True beauty is the gift of God that lives within us and makes our virtues shine." With our sassy, bumpin' and grindin' dance routines, and the clappin' and stompin' of our step routines, I don't think any casual observer would conclude that our sorority was about God or virtue. What we did get right was sisterhood—cultivating a community of love and trust.

LCC taught me about leadership and loyalty. To display our group loyalty, we often wore our sorority colors of red and white or customized T-shirts that included our emblem, a single-stem red rose. The beauty of our connection was cultivated in our indoctrination process known as pledging. During this thirty-day period, members were allowed to talk only to each other. There was public shame and embarrassment when a pledge was caught communicating with a boyfriend or a best friend who was not a part of our organization. The sisterhood came first.

This training process also included some humiliation. After I joined, the first thing our big sisters did was to assign each of the pledges a line name that was supposed to characterize our personality but was often degrading. Each morning before the school bell rang, we lined up for "roll call" as a way of showing our solidarity, and this routine provided entertainment for the rest of the school. One of my long-time friends was a tap dancer, so they named her "Kermit the Frog." When her name was called, she proceeded to tap and sing, "Happy Feet. I've got those happy feet." My big sisters couldn't find anything particularly right or wrong with another line sister or me, so they named us after the cartoon characters Beavis and Butthead. I do believe I was the latter.

Each pledge also had to make (not buy) a white pillow—trimmed in white lace and with a single-stem red rose attached. Although I did not know how to sew, I had to invest the time to craft it to our big sisters' approval, and we were required to carry it along with our school books. Our pillows were a constant reminder that our sisters were always with us. Together we met every demand, denied our own desires, offered a helping hand to any line sister in need, and made a bond with our new sisters. We completely made fools of ourselves in public, but we did it all together. In spite of the ridicule, at the end of pledging I felt a sense of accomplishment and belonging. I had earned my place, and I was not alone. LCC was my community, and while I wouldn't use the same training tactics now, those early lessons in loyalty did prepare me for where I was going.

THE HELEN SHEFFIELD JUNIOR FEDERATED GIRLS CLUB

At the same time that I was pondering joining the sisterhood of LCC during my freshmen year, I was also invited to participate in a four-year debutante program with the Helen Sheffield Junior Federated Girls Club. Unlike programs for organizations where class or sorority affiliations became determining factors, this program was offered to any African American girl with potential. When I looked around in the first meeting at the others who had joined, I noticed that we all had decent grades and didn't get into major trouble. But not everyone who started with us finished the program. For some, their character didn't stick. For others, pursuing boys was more important than tending to their grades or to the commitments we made to the organization.

This club was a community where God and virtue were elevated, where I was required to read Scripture aloud for the first time outside of a sunrise Easter service, and where I practiced singing "Lift Every Voice and Sing." It was where I learned about ethics, character development, and public service. The organization was also dedicated to preparing us for womanhood by providing etiquette training, forming a sisterhood, and encouraging our hopes and dreams for the future.

For four years, we attended monthly meetings that included remembering and appreciating the contributions of civil rights activists, educators, and female pioneers, while also honoring our unique African American heritage. Our community and culture were embodied in our pledge:

> On my honor, I pledge: to do unto others as I would have them do unto me; to face life squarely; to have a definite plan and purpose in life; to strive to seek the highest ideals for my soul and live up to them; to always be dependable; to learn the secret of team work; to have faith in God, faith in others and faith in myself; to cultivate thrift, honesty, truthfulness and reliance; to realize that persistent good will break down barriers; to be honest to myself and true to my country; to be ready to "Lift as I Climb."

Our leader, Ms. Geraldine Zimmerman, was a Christian and a lifelong member of the National Association for the Advancement of Colored People (NAACP). She affirmed our existence, taught us to respect our elders, and insisted on our excellence. This community was about honor and respect. It was about living our lives on purpose and having high standards for ourselves and for each other. It was about growing in faith and truth. Our conversations and instruction always centered on words like *us*, *we*, and *our people*. Together, we would lift as we climbed.

In this community, we were taught that being black and being a woman was something worth loving. And I *loved* everything about being a black girl. It was not until I left home that I realized that loving and affirming blackness was not the norm in America. Things were quite different in the "real world." I'm so glad that my identity was formed and shaped in this community, because when messages from the world aimed to attack my womanhood, my blackness, my skin tone, or my hair, I simply rejected those lies. The people from my own community loved and cared for me, and they told me the truth about myself.

THERE'S NO PLACE LIKE HOME

In spite of the love and affection I received in Orangeburg, South Carolina, I wanted to get out. My reason for leaving was simple: Orangeburg lacked opportunity. Over the years, through road trips to visit family members who had participated in the Great Migration (the twentieth-century exodus of almost six million African Americans from the South to northern and western cities), I had experienced the wonder of multiple cities in New York. While in middle and high school, I had opportunities to visit big cities with the Orangeburg Junior Olympic Track Club. These experiences affirmed my resolve to go places and to see the world. I wanted a job that paid well, and I wanted adventure. When I left Orangeburg, it didn't even have a Walmart!

Although I come from a small town and still refer to myself as a small-town girl, Orangeburg was simply too small for me. By the time I was eighteen, I had outgrown it like a teenage boy outgrows last season's sneakers. I needed something that was a better fit. I wanted more opportunities because I had hope for a better future.

We all leave home for different reasons. The first time Moses left home—the place where he was born—it was not by his own choosing but because of his mother's survival instincts. When he entered the palace, it wasn't lost on anyone—not on Moses or his family, Pharaoh or his daughter, the Egyptians or the Hebrews—that Moses was not an Egyptian. Although he was not raised with his biological family, he continued to identify with them.

The Bible records:

> One day, after Moses had grown up, he went out to where his own people were and watched them at their hard labor. He saw an Egyptian beating a Hebrew, one of his own people. Looking this way and that and seeing no one, he killed the Egyptian and hid him in the sand. The next day he went out and saw two Hebrews fighting. He asked the one in the wrong, "Why are you hitting your fellow Hebrew?" (Exodus 2:11-13)

Moses empathized with and cared about his own Hebrew people. With them he shared an identity, culture, and history. His origin was an intentional act of God, and that was important to Moses. When he noticed the injustices imposed on the Hebrews by the Egyptians, he took action. He also wanted his fellow Hebrews to do right by each other and be better for themselves.

The Egyptian palace was not Moses' forever home. His righteous anger expressed in an unrighteous way—killing an Egyptian—forced him to leave his second home and flee to Midian. There he found and married his wife, and they began to raise a family. But Midian was not his forever home either. We soon learn that God was calling him out of that place also.

The Hebrew home and culture, the Egyptian palace full of wealth and power, and the land of shepherds in Midian became training grounds to prepare Moses for his life's purpose. Each of them shaped his identity. Community is a place.

Many of us who trust and follow God are, like Moses, destined in some way to wander and sojourn in this strange land we call earth. Our physical homes change, but community is not only a place. Remember that "leaders are not shaped in isolation.... God deliberately and intentionally shapes the leader's heart through community." Community is about people.

Since I've left Orangeburg and have experienced so many losses of loved ones, I have often felt like a restless wanderer all alone in this big world. I used to visualize myself like that scared little girl Dorothy who crashed into the Land of Oz, looking around and saying to her dog and only friend, Toto, "We're not in Kansas anymore."

When I think about community being the formation that happens among people, the theme song for the classic sitcom *Cheers* immediately comes to mind: "Sometimes you want to go where everybody knows your name—and they're always glad you came." Once upon a time, that special place for me was in the community of Orangeburg, South Carolina. I suspect that for Moses that special place was among his biological family, perhaps with his adopted mother, and then with the family he found in Midian. For the fictional character Dorothy, it was with her Uncle Henry and Auntie Em—although she didn't realize it until she left home. What Dorothy learned has also been my life lesson: we often appreciate our formative communities most after we've moved on.

SHAPING OUR COMMUNITIES

By God's grace, in my wanderings I have found intimate friends and an extended spiritual family. But I've also learned that we each have a responsibility to create the types of communities we need to sustain ourselves on this faith journey. Like Moses in the Egyptian palace, we may sometimes live in one place while resonating with another. Sometimes we might feel as if we don't fit any place at all.

As a black woman and a competent leader who is somewhat scholarly, somewhat cool, and somewhat loud, I don't quite fit anywhere within the American evangelical church. I was also raised as an American patriot, attended the Naval Academy, and served as a Marine Corps officer, and as I grow in spiritual maturity that patriotism can easily conflict with my Christian faith, personal ethics, and values.

I'm beginning to understand that such a sense of homelessness is the hallmark of a godly leader. Homelessness is not necessarily being alone or experiencing loneliness, for great leaders are often surrounded by people. Homelessness is a weariness of spirit. It is the constant friction and tension of being misquoted or misunderstood. It is the restlessness that sets in from being a sojourner on this earth. It also moves us to reject the ways of this world to become more like Jesus, the prophet who was without honor in his own home (Mark 6:4) and who did not have a place to lay his head (Matthew 8:20).

> We each have a responsibility to create the types of communities we need to sustain ourselves on this faith journey.

As we wander and wait for Jesus' return, we are reminded that our place in time and our history continue to shape us. The lyrics of the Black National Anthem remind me of a long spiritual journey and communal need for accountability:

God of our weary years, God of our silent tears,
Thou who has brought us thus far on the way;
Thou who has by Thy might, Led us into the light,
Keep us forever in the path, we pray.

Lest our feet stray from the places, our God, where we
    met Thee,
Lest, our hearts drunk with the wine of the world, we
    forget Thee;
Shadowed beneath Thy hand, may we forever stand,
True to our God, true to our native land.

When the people and values that shape my diverse communities are in conflict with each other, I must consider: Will I remain true to my God or true to the native land or continent in which my ancestors were born, or will I remain true to the native land or country in which I was born? My native land wants me to remain true to the American philosophy that I have been taught in my formative years. On the other hand, my people—the black community—have a history of being oppressed by the land in which many of us were born. Where should my loyalties lie, knowing all of that? The black community has also been stripped of our African culture, history, and traditions, and I want to learn what values have been lost from that culture and to understand what values are important to hold on to.

Discernment for the American Christian is determining what is actually of God and what is true only to our native land. Believe it or not, American Christianity looks quite different depending on where and how you worship on Sunday mornings, what stories you read, what voices you listen to, and who you call friend. Our various community shapers can be in conflict with each other, so remaining true to God requires that we analyze the sacred community—the shaping grounds, including what or who is missing from those spaces. Affirming our identity in Christ means that we must wrestle with our community shapers to accept, celebrate, cultivate, and then share what individually makes us unique.

Community is about the places that shape us. Orangeburg, South Carolina, is where I come from. Community is about the people who shape us. When I had the opportunity to deliver the student address at my graduation from Gordon-Conwell Theological Seminary Charlotte, I told my family and friends, "I take you with me wherever I go." Community is who you roll with on this journey called life.

Community is also the environments that we intentionally cultivate and the people we invite to form and shape them. Creating culture and cultivating community is a continuous act of discipline. If you desire to have lasting influence and to implement real change, this is an internal wrestling you must be willing to do, a risk you must be willing to take, and a skill you must learn. Your life may look very different from mine or that of Moses. You have your own stories, relationships, and experiences. The work of spiritual formation requires that you pay attention to how God wants to shape your community.

TRUTH IS: Community is a place, the people, culture, time, and history that influence us. It shapes and grows us into the people we are. When our community shapers are in conflict, we must wrestle with them so God can use our whole life experiences to honor him.

REFLECTION QUESTION: Can you describe your community shapers? In what ways might they be in conflict?

SCRIPTURE MEDITATION:

> A person's steps are directed by the LORD.
> How then can anyone understand their own way?
> (Proverbs 20:24)

PERSONAL AFFIRMATION: God determines my steps and directs the path of my life; therefore, I can trust his purposes for the community he allows to shape me.

CALL TO ACTION: Take some time this week to list the various communities that have shaped you. What did you learn from them (good or bad)? How has God used those experiences in your life?

PRAYER: God, you are the Creator of all things. You have caused humans to populate the whole earth. You determine the times set before us and the places where we live. You do this so that we can seek you and reach out to you, understanding that you are not far from any of us (Acts 17:26-27). When my shaping communities are in conflict, and I am challenged about which way to go, help me to remain true to you. In Jesus' name, amen.

TWEET: We have a responsibility to create the types of communities we need to sustain ourselves on this faith journey. @asistasjourney #ASojournersTruth

CHAPTER FOUR

PURPOSE

TRUTH IS, WINNERS DON'T QUIT ON THEMSELVES

For the cramped bewildered years we went
to school to learn to know the reasons why and the
answers to and the people who and the places where
and the days when, in memory of the bitter
hours when we discovered we were black
and poor and small and different.

MARGARET WALKER, "FOR MY PEOPLE"

want to see a chaplain," I said in my timid voice, yet with a quiet resistance that burned deep within me. I knew the power of those words when I spoke them during the Plebe Summer of 1998.

Plebe Summer is the Naval Academy's six-week indoctrination period for freshmen, also known as plebes. Plebes were defined in our study manual, *Reef Points*, as "that insignificant thing that gets all the sympathy and chow [food] from home." So the message was clear from day one of training: We didn't have a right to call ourselves leaders. We would first learn how to follow. Our leadership training was conducted by second-class (rising juniors) and first-class (rising seniors) students (also known as upper-class midshipmen). From them, we received no sympathy.

WE WERE BLACK AND DIFFERENT

When you undertake a responsibility like attending the United States Naval Academy, you expect that it will be difficult. In many ways, you welcome the challenge. You understand that it will be hard for everyone and that this great risk will yield greater life rewards. But I was not like the majority of students who attended the United States Naval Academy. I was not white. I was not male. I was not from a wealthy family. I did not have a legacy. I was one of only three African Americans in my platoon of approximately forty plebes.

By the time we were halfway through the summer training period, all three of the African Americans had received D's in our professional and military performance. These grades were arbitrary, so when I went to review my performance report with the company officer, I was confused to read negative remarks from the upperclassmen who made claims about my disrespect or lack of table manners. Since I didn't know charges would be levied against me, I was prepared neither to own them nor to defend myself. I was silent. I said a few "Yes, Sirs," nodded my head respectfully, signed the form, and walked out.

I guess the upperclassmen neglected to inform our company officer about the private moments when they were disrespectful of people like me. I still remember the day that my anger and bitterness started to kick in. I was coming out of the female head (the public restroom on a military base) and dutifully squared my corners with high knees, and a motivated "Go Navy, Sir. Beat Army, Sir," as we had been trained to do every time we turned a corner. Then I heard her voice blaring down the hallway.

"Sistrunk, STOP!" I froze and waited for her—this blond and motivated second-class midshipman who was responsible for training the plebes in my company—to catch up to me.

"I don't like you," she said. "You don't deserve to be here at my school. You know what I'm gonna do, Sistrunk? Imma keep writing you bad paperwork, and you know what's gonna happen? That's going to build up a file, and eventually, they gonna kick you outta here. You understand what I'm saying?"

At the Naval Academy, I was afforded five basic responses when receiving correction from an upper-class midshipmen or senior officer: (1) "Yes Ma'am," (2) "No Ma'am," (3) "No excuse Ma'am," (4) "Aye, Aye Ma'am," and (5) "I'll find out Ma'am." These responses were "designed to facilitate an understanding on the part of each plebe of his/her responsibility to respond to seniors in an alert, direct, and unequivocal manner, as well as the necessity to take full responsibility for one's actions." So I replied to the second-class midshipman's threat the only way I was allowed: "Ma'am, Yes, Ma'am!"

I didn't fully understand that I was being discriminated against in the hallway, but I became keenly aware when I left my company officer's office that the racism and the railroading had begun. I also understood that I had to learn this game and learn it fast if I was to survive—and I certainly intended to survive.

None of the upper-class midshipmen understood that when I arrived I was mentally prepared to graduate. The Naval Academy is an institution of higher learning that has a mission for moral, mental, and physical development. I had intestinal fortitude, and I didn't shy away from challenges.

A PURPOSEFUL PATH

The Naval Academy recruited me because I was a competitive athlete. When their track coach started the recruitment process during my junior year of high school, I had no intention of attending "the boat school." I literally threw the literature away for a year, not knowing that the coach continued to pursue my mother. Because of my mother's persuasion, my guidance counselor's wisdom, and my history teacher's encouragement, I completed the application process, and I started to pray about this decision.

I received the acceptance letter to attend the Naval Academy Preparatory School in the spring of my senior year on the day after the state track championship. By that time, I had broken the school record in my specialty event, the one-hundred-meter hurdles. I had won first place in the state for the same event, and in the spring of my junior year, our girls and boys track teams won the state championship.

College acceptance letters and scholarships were rolling in. When I saw the envelope from the Naval Academy on my grandmother's kitchen table, I aggressively tore it open to read the words, "You are accepted . . ." Before it registered in my mind, I started to cry.

As we follow Moses' story, we learn that he found his purpose at the burning bush. That was where he began his faith journey. That was where he had a miraculous encounter with God that he didn't fully understand. In the same way, God spoke to me when I opened that letter. I didn't know why my tears were flowing. Attending this school was not something I had dreamed about or asked God for. The opportunity was put before me, and I simply decided to take a look. This was God's prompting—my "this is the way, now walk in it" moment (see Isaiah 30:21). It was as if God had purposed this path for me. On that day, I knew that I would go to the United States Naval Academy, and I knew that I would graduate.

I loved the practical reality of the situation: the Academy would offer me a full scholarship, pay me to go to school, and guarantee a promising career upon graduation. I was the oldest of three children in a family with little monetary means, and I didn't want my parents to worry about financially supporting me. Attending this school was my first step to financial freedom. Graduating college debt-free with a career that pays well and offers upward mobility is a great starting point for any young adult. I knew that the choice to attend the Naval Academy would change my life forever.

The Naval Academy chose me, and I chose them among other prestigious institutions where I had been accepted and received scholarship offers, including Virginia Tech, North Carolina State, and North Carolina A&T University. I also chose them because my mother, her brother, and my maternal grandfather had all served in the military. I looked forward to having a career where I could be a public servant and travel the world with my friends.

Not once did I think about quitting the Naval Academy. There was simply too much to lose. And I certainly was not going to let any of them—the girl in the hallway or her friends—mess

> *I had every intention of finishing what I started.*

up this opportunity for me. From the time I set foot on the Naval Academy's campus, I had every intention of finishing what I started. I would work to make the Naval Academy *my* school too.

IN THE CHAPLAIN'S OFFICE

When I said, "I want to see a chaplain," I understood that the upperclassmen were trying to get me to quit. I was learning the game. I paid attention to the things they whispered in hallways and the code they used to communicate as if I were not in the room. I asked because it was within my rights, and I knew they were required to comply without question.

As I was escorted to the chapel, one of the upperclassmen yelled out to his peer, "Did we get her?" My escort replied with glee, "Almost!" They didn't understand that I was only looking for some relief—the kind that all of us need when we are doing something that is hard and purposeful.

I entered the office of Chaplain Diana Meehan, and we sat quietly for a few minutes. I couldn't quite articulate my feelings. Besides, I didn't really know whose side she was on or what authority she had, and I didn't want to spill my guts to some stranger.

She offered me words of encouragement and asked if I wanted to make a phone call. I picked up the phone and anxiously dialed my mother. Mom didn't answer, so we waited a few minutes and I tried again. No answer.

I thought about the other phone numbers that I had memorized. Talking to my maternal grandmother in a moment like this was out of the question, so I decided to call my mom's sister, Aunt Linda. Linda is the free spirit of the family. She is the laugh-out-loud, life-of-any-party, crank-up-the-music, cook-the-food-and-bring-the-drinks-so-everyone-can-have-a-good-time-on-the-street-corner type of person. People know her for her hospitality. I thought she might be able to lift my spirits, but when I heard her familiar voice on the other end of the line with her drawn out, jolly "Hellooo," I lost it. Immediately I became aware that I was homesick. I missed Aunt Linda. I missed my mother, my family, and my community. I missed knowing without a shadow of doubt that I was known, loved, and accepted.

As my lips trembled and tears welled up in my eyes, I had to force the words through the lump that was grabbing at my throat, so I spoke softly. "Aunt Linda, this is Tasha. They don't want me here . . . ," and I began to cry out loud.

Another thing my Aunt Linda is known for is crying without notice. On that day, however, she didn't join in with me. There was only a long silence on the line. I'm so glad that she was out of character. I was out of character too. There we sat—she on one end of the line, and I on the other—comforting each other in our silence, pondering, *What do we do now?*

After a few seconds that felt more like minutes, my aunt mustered only a few words, "It will be okay, baby." She never said anything foolish like, "Come on home" or "Why don't you quit?" We both knew that I was capable and that the idea of quitting was simply unacceptable. She also understood that I had left home for better opportunities. And since all the other college slots were filled, and all the other scholarships were gone, what was left to go back home to?

Our conversation was over quickly. We said, "I love you," and I was about to hang up when I added, "Aunt Linda, please don't tell my momma that I called." I was so thankful that my mother was not home that day. She would have needlessly worried about me for the rest of the summer.

By the end of that call, I had been comforted. I received the relief that I so desperately needed. As I sat in the chair of that chaplain's office, I remembered Ms. Zimmerman, my leader in the Helen Sheffield Junior Federated Girls Club, and how she recounted the NAACP's fight for human rights. I remembered the closing words of "Lift Every Voice and Sing": "Let us march on 'til victory is won!" I remembered that my father and mother told me over and over again that I could be or do anything I wanted, and that understanding would only be realized if I worked hard. I remembered who I was, where I had come from, the black people who had gone on before me, and I began to rise up in myself again.

I left the chaplain's office knowing that I would not be moved. It was the first and last time I cried that summer.

UNQUALIFIED AND AWAKENED

I suppose the day at my grandmother's kitchen table and the day in the chaplain's office could have both been considered spiritual encounters, although neither were as glamorous as Moses' burning bush experience. When God made his purpose for Moses clear, he was in the desert on a mountain top speaking to a bush that was on fire but did not burn up. Moses' purpose was to go back to Egypt—the empire where he had been raised—to bring a message to the new pharaoh (Exodus 3:1–4:17).

God called Moses out by name, and Moses answered, "Here I am."

God informed Moses of who God was and the work he was doing. God was concerned about Moses' people, the enslaved Hebrews. God would fulfill his purpose and promise to them, and he would put an end to their suffering.

Moses would be God's agent for accomplishing this work, but Moses was unsure about himself and this call. He had questions. He asked, "Who am I that I should go to Pharaoh and bring the Israelites out of Egypt?" (3:11).

Then God reminded Moses of a few key truths regarding his purpose: "I will be with you" (3:12). *Because* I *am sending you,* I *will finish the work.*

In spite of these truths, Moses still had doubts and questioned himself and God: "Suppose I go to the Israelites and say to them, 'The God of your fathers has sent me to you,' and they ask me, 'What is his name?' Then what shall I tell them?" (3:13).

"What if they do not believe me or listen to me and say, 'The LORD did not appear to you'?" (4:1).

"I have never been eloquent, neither in the past nor since you have spoken to your servant. I am slow of speech and tongue" (4:10).

"Pardon your servant, Lord. Please send someone else" (4:13).

But for every question, every doubt, and every obstacle, God had an answer. For every person who didn't believe, God showed himself as true. Moses would not fulfill his purpose in his own strength. The God of his ancestors—Abraham, Isaac, and Jacob—would be with him. The God who simply referred to himself as "I AM WHO I AM" (3:14). Some scholars translate this as "I will be what I will be." I can hear a black preacher in the back of my mind right now reminding the congregation that "God is! He is everything you need him to be ..."

> For every question, every doubt, and every obstacle, God had an answer.

On that day in the hallway when that blond upperclassman made clear her intentions for my life, I needed God as my peace. In my company officer's office, I needed God as an advocate. In the chaplain's office, I needed his comfort. Moses needed God to strengthen his resolve. Then he needed the great I AM to work a miracle and provide a voice box. God is, he does, and he did all of this to fulfill his good purposes.

Like me, Moses was positioned for his purpose, but in some ways he wasn't prepared. As a matter of fact, he was unqualified and he knew it. What God did for Moses at the burning bush and what he did for me in that chaplain's office was awaken us to our purpose and to the possibilities. The preparation would come later in the training and in our "long obedience in the same direction," as author Eugene Peterson puts it. However, walking in our purpose begins with miraculous encounters. It begins with a subtle shifting in our present reality, a look back to the place where we have come from, a challenge to answer the present call, and an invitation to pursue a promising future, where the great I AM has sworn to lead us on the way. Walking in our purpose means that we cannot quit!

PURPOSE IN PRESENCE

When people start to think about their purpose, they often begin with a basic question like, "How do I know what God wants?" The answer is pretty simple: Ask him. Then wait and listen for his response. We learn from Moses' example that we find our purpose when we take the risk of being present with God. God was on that mountain, and Moses was intrigued so he walked over to meet with him at the burning bush. He accepted the invitation to enter God's presence.

As I wrote in my book *Mentor for Life*, "Sometimes we are not present because we are trying to play God—we move too fast and try to accomplish too much without acknowledging the limitations of our humanity and the constraints of our time. . . . So when we have the opportunity to sit in silence before God or be fully present with others, we are uncomfortable." Moses was uncomfortable, but he was also on holy ground, and he stayed long enough to listen.

Standing on the holy ground of God's presence gives us the right perspective. When we come face-to-face with God, we also come face-to-face with ourselves, and we become aware of our own sinfulness, weakness, pride, and human limitations. It moves us to desire *less of me and more of God*, and it opens our understanding to consider God's way of working in this world. So, we must be present with God if we are ever to know our purpose.

> We must be present with God if we are ever to know our purpose.

Choosing to follow God and become a disciple of Jesus is an act of faith and risk, as well as discomfort. This movement leads us into the holiness of walking in our purpose, understanding our call to action, and knowing our work.

I never doubted myself or my abilities until I went to the Naval Academy. I was a person who always worked hard and grew accustomed to having success as a result of that hard work. Yet in the four years of training at the Annapolis bay, the humbling work began for me and several of my friends. It was "the bitter hours when we discovered we were black and poor and small and different." The upperclassmen tried to tear us down. I was challenged to become something I was not or to reject the person I was. There were times then when I doubted.

In the seasons of forgetfulness, I remembered my home and my community. I sought the presence of the burning bush—the one who had prepared my heart at my grandmother's kitchen table and in that chaplain's office—and I remembered the truth that had been so firmly planted at home. My purpose to become a disciple of Christ and a leader of people was affirmed.

Knowing your purpose and walking in it is never a matter of your worth or human qualifications, because your purpose isn't about *you*. Instead, purpose is about believing in God, embracing his kingdom mission, and understanding that he can use anyone to fulfill *his* good purposes—even you and me.

Moses was able to live with purpose because he sought the presence of God, and there he found the promises God had for him. God said to Moses, "I will be with you. And this will be the sign to you that it is I who have sent you: When you have brought the people out of Egypt, you will worship God on this mountain" (Exodus 3:12). There are two promises wrapped up in this verse:

- God will be with you wherever you go. God made this promise to Moses and later to Joshua (Joshua 1:9), and he makes the same promise to you if you seek his face and walk in his way (Psalm 139:7-10).

- God will fulfill the purpose he has for you. The word *when* in the English translation signifies accomplishment. God will finish the good work that he initiates through you. The apostle Paul gives this same word of encouragement and confirmation to the church in Philippi (Philippians 1:6).

Our responsibility as leaders and servants of God is to trust his purpose and will for our lives, to pay attention, to obey the promptings of his calling, and to never give up.

TRUTH IS: God has a purpose for each of us, and he often affirms that purpose over time and through our experiences. Our responsibility is to trust God, follow where he leads, and never give up.

REFLECTION QUESTION: What purpose does God have for your life? How has he shaped you to fulfill that purpose from the very beginning?

SCRIPTURE MEDITATION: God's word to the prophet Jeremiah:

> Before I formed you in the womb I knew you,
>> before you were born I set you apart;
>> I appointed you as a prophet to the nations.
>> (Jeremiah 1:4-5)

PERSONAL AFFIRMATION: God has a purpose for my life; therefore, I must be attentive to his calling and obey.

CALL TO ACTION: Ask the trusted people in your community what work of God and what purpose they have witnessed operating in your life. This will provide great encouragement when the obedience and work get hard.

PRAYER: Lord, I thank you that I can take you at your Word. I can trust that because you do not change, you will clearly reveal your purpose and allow me to walk in it until the very end. You did this for Moses, and you will do it for me. In Jesus' name, amen.

TWEET: Knowing your purpose and walking in it is never a matter of your worth or human qualifications. @asistasjourney #ASojournersTruth

PART TWO

*For the L*ORD *your God is . . . mighty and awesome,*

who shows no partiality and accepts no bribes.

DEUTERONOMY 10:17

None of us develops our worldview in a vacuum. Our God-given identities, history, and culture all shape our rules of engagement.

Black. Woman. No matter how you slice it, I come from a marginalized group. This truth doesn't change because I am a Christian. Sometimes the church is just as guilty of the racism and sexism that is prominent in the world, but my God does not show partiality.

The biblical exodus narrative has given generations of African Americans hope for a freedom that is never voluntarily given but must always be demanded. In part two we make a sojourn to consider Moses' demands for freedom, and we witness the deliverance at the Red Sea. This biblical history motivates me to demand freedom, to serve humanity, and to tell the truth that "there is neither Jew nor Gentile, neither slave nor free, nor is there male and female, for you are all one in Christ Jesus" (Galatians 3:28).

We can miss our purpose if we don't observe God's hand at work throughout history. God is on a mission to redeem all things, including us. Surrender. Give yourself permission to interrogate your life in light of the society, culture, and family in which you were raised. Allow history to become your teacher.

CHAPTER FIVE

CONSCIOUSNESS

TRUTH IS, IT'S TIME
TO WAKE UP

*We the people of this new generation highly
resolve that those who sacrificed before us shall not
have sacrificed in vain. Let justice roll on.*

ELIZABETH PERKINS, IN
LET JUSTICE ROLL DOWN

I hate when folks are denied the opportunity to exercise their
God-given dominion on earth. The idea of supremacy—the
right to power for a select few—has resulted in oppression that has
negatively affected generations of people of color. God has allowed
me to bear witness to this injustice in my generation.

In addition to its rich culture, my hometown's history includes
racism, segregation, and generational poverty. Orangeburg's most no-
torious history reveals the atrocities of Jim Crow and the town's resistance to the civil rights movement. Learning this history has caused
me to become more intentional in my work toward biblical justice.

THE ORANGEBURG MASSACRE

When I was a child, my family shopped at the Piggly Wiggly
grocery store. In the shopping center adjacent to the store, there
was an old bowling alley marked by a faded red, white, and blue

marquee for Floyd's All-Star Bowling Lanes. Although the bowling alley had been closed many years prior, we often used the parking lot. And there, at the front of the building, were three black and white pictures clearly displayed in the window.

I learned from my mother that the photos served as a memorial to three young, black men: Samuel Hammond Jr. (eighteen years old), Delano Middleton (seventeen years old), and Henry Smith (eighteen years old), who were murdered in what would become known as the Orangeburg Massacre. This event occurred a little over a decade before I was born, and whenever I asked my mother specific questions about it, she would simply reply, "I was there," and then change the subject.

The bowling alley was previously owned by Harry Floyd, who, despite the passage of the 1964 Civil Rights Act, decided not to let Negroes bowl in his establishment. Henry Smith was part of a growing student movement to desegregate the only bowling alley within a twenty-mile radius of the town. Henry and many of his fellow students were becoming more conscious of the systemic injustices that denied black people access to the same rights and privileges that white citizens so easily enjoyed. Only white American citizens could sit wherever they wanted on a bus, eat at lunch counters, enter through the front doors of businesses, purchase homes in the neighborhoods of their choosing, or have their military personnel return home as heroes and not as second-class citizens. The standard of Jim Crow dehumanized blacks, and now they demanded change.

What began as nonviolent protests and formal grievances escalated into confusion. The college students grew particularly angry about the physical abuse and violence the police imposed on female students. First-hand accounts document these shameful beatings. On the night of the massacre, Louise Kelly Cawley—a pregnant married woman and senior college student—resisted arrest out of fear for her life. She was severely beaten by a cop, and she miscarried her baby the following week.

On February 28, 1968, sixty-six state patrolmen, twenty-five South Carolina Law Enforcement Division officers, and nearly four hundred National Guardsmen were on duty in this small town. The students assembled to protest and set a bonfire that night as an act of resistance. Nearly 150 students were lingering outside Lowman Hall at State College (now South Carolina State University) when the police opened fire into the crowd. The police shooting resulted in the deaths of Delano, Henry, and Samuel and the injury of twenty-seven others.

This massacre was the first of its kind on any American college campus.

This is an American story, and it is the shared legacy of the Orangeburg Wilkinson High School, Claflin University, and South Carolina State University students who began protesting against segregation in the 1960s.

Every time we drove by that abandoned bowling alley, I was reminded of this history and how the police abused their power. It was also not lost on me that young people—seventeen- and eighteen-year-old students—demanded a way out of their oppression. Hearing stories like these as a child helped me understand that taking a stand against oppression and struggling to effect positive change was not outside of me. As I became more conscious, I realized that fighting for equity, justice, and upward mobility for people of color in particular is very much a part of who I am.

Consciousness is more than knowing the facts; it is more than having an awareness of cultural issues. Surely it starts there, but when attended to it grows into an inner stirring prompting a necessary response to that knowledge. As a black child, I knew that I would join the fight for freedom.

A CALL TO CONSCIENCE

Stories like those of the Orangeburg Massacre raised my awareness about the black experience in America, particularly in the South. I've lived in the Carolinas for most of my life so I know that South Carolina is a stubborn state, often stuck in old ways. The state is famous for denying the dignity of its African American citizens. This history cannot be ignored, and it is only magnified when we evaluate how that trajectory continues today.

Injustices affect the lives of real people. We can all become more conscious of this truth. Hearing the stories of people of color informs us and hopefully shapes our understanding of the racial and economic disparities that are so prevalent in our society. Many young people working for justice today refer to this heightened consciousness as "being woke," and they often encourage fellow sojourners to "stay woke." You see, raising one's consciousness requires intentionality and persistence. It requires the external work of education through continuous learning and the internal work of humility and self-awareness, while acknowledging our personal histories, privileges, and biases. Consciousness is not simply an intellectual or internal pursuit. As a Christian, raising one's consciousness is also a spiritual pursuit that leads us to righteous actions.

> Raising one's consciousness is also a spiritual pursuit that leads us to righteous actions.

I have learned this from paying attention to the life, legacy, and leadership of Dr. Martin Luther King Jr. To better understand the world in which both he and my mother were raised, and to pick up the torch of righteousness from their generation, I frequently visit his story and his words.

In the introduction to a book of King's speeches titled *A Call to Conscience*, Andrew Young, who worked with King in the Southern

Christian Leadership Conference, writes, "Martin's voice was more than the communication of intellectual ideals and spiritual vision. It was a call for action, action which he personally led.... [Martin] saw leadership as a process of relating the daily plight of humankind to the eternal truths of creation." Likewise, as Christian parents, pastors, professors, public servants, or people in the marketplace, it is not enough for us to have kind words and thoughts toward our neighbors. We must personally lead our brothers and sisters into righteous action that connects our daily work and acts of service to the greater, eternal, and redemptive work God is doing throughout the world.

WHAT I LEARNED AT HOME

I didn't realize it right away, but this consciousness—this call to freedom fighting, leadership, and change—was already at work in my heart by the time I was a teenager. The artifacts are evident in my father's home. If you were to visit his modest apartment, you would find several display cases in his living room. The shelves are filled with awards representing his children's accomplishments. He began this record keeping with my mother, who had commemorations of her own.

Shortly after her death, I finally mustered the energy to go through her things. Among her organized files I found a red folder with crumbled edges. On the front, her cursive handwriting etched out my name, *Natasha*, in faded black marker. Within that folder I found copies of my awards, pictures, newspaper clippings, vaccination records, college acceptance letters, ceremonial programs, some speeches I had given, and even a few scholarship essays—all artifacts from a time long past.

Every now and then, I revisit that folder because I want to remember the girl that I was, the things she cared about, and how deeply she wanted to change the world. I want to remember the hopes and dreams she had for her future. That's what artifacts do. They raise our consciousness by reminding us of who we are and where we are going. This type of reflection is an important spiritual practice for leaders and influencers of change.

Edgar H. Schein writes, "The bottom line for leaders is that if they do not become conscious of the culture in which they are embedded, those cultures will manage them. Cultural understanding is desirable for all of us, but it is essential for leaders if they are to lead." Cultural consciousness is necessary if we are to become people who stand against oppression and change the world. We must be aware of our own culture, the diverse cultures around us, and the ways in which those cultures intersect, collide, and impact each other.

Artifacts describe the culture and environments in which we live, and they also provide an informed history for us to analyze. Schein writes that artifacts require us to ask the question, "What is going on here?" A visitor to my father's home, for example, would quickly understand that he values his children's achievements.

> *Cultural consciousness is necessary if we are to become people who stand against oppression and change the world.*

For years, South Carolina has placed a high value on celebrating the Confederate flag. As I peered through the yellowed, coffee-stained pages in my mother's folder, I found a college scholarship essay where I addressed this issue:

> I understand that the flag represents bravery of the confederate soldiers. . . . This is only one sign of representation, however. The flag also represents slavery . . . the idea that blacks are still inferior to whites. . . . That may be your personal belief, and if so, wear the flag on your t-shirt; hang it on

your front lawn; or put it on your license plate. That is no reason to disrespect African American citizens every time they pass the Statehouse, a historical government building for all citizens. Flying the flag at the Statehouse means that the state does not believe that all people are created equal. . . . Racism is a deeply rooted problem that needs to be taken care of immediately. Any small thing we can do to resolve this problem, we should do. If that means removing the flag from the state capital, then so be it. . . . I respect our history and understand that we cannot change the past. We can, however, change the future. People need to come together and resolve the issue.

I was eighteen years old when I wrote those words. In 1997, I was hopeful for a solution that would honor our history *and* the dignity of the black citizens of South Carolina.

Over the years, however, I watched as the state continued to elevate this artifact. Even the loss of millions of tourism dollars didn't change the lawmakers' position. I understand now that the Confederate flag in all its glory represents an American culture that some people still long for—where blacks were enslaved and subservient to whites, and people of color wouldn't dare demand their own freedoms.

For nearly two decades after I wrote that essay, the Confederate flag continued to fly at the South Carolina statehouse grounds. The first time I saw it removed was on June 27, 2015, when the African American woman activist Bree Newsome was hoisted by a white man named James Ian Tyson over the fence that enclosed the flag. Tyson stood watch as Newsome climbed the flagpole. She removed the flag and publicly declared, "You come against me with hatred, oppression, and violence. I come against you in the name of God. This flag comes down today." As she descended from the pole to face her arrest, she recited Psalm 27 and Psalm 23. This act of non-violent protest preceded the South Carolina House vote to officially remove the flag on July 9, 2015. In a move of political expediency, then-governor Nikki Haley signed the bill on July 10, 2015.

PAINFUL CATALYSTS

Just a month prior to this historic decision, on June 17, 2015, white supremacist Dylan Roof murdered nine African Americans in the sanctuary of Emanuel AME Church in Charleston, South Carolina, less than a two-hour drive from my hometown. In addition to the swastika on his jacket, there were several photographs online of Roof posing with the Confederate flag. While some minimize the negative message the Confederate flag sends, I think Roof understood what the artifact communicated.

This massacre left me shocked—numb even—because it was too close to home. I have family members who knew people that died in Emanuel AME Church on that Wednesday night. One of the deceased, Sharonda Coleman-Singleton, was a graduate of South Carolina State University. I was overwhelmed with grief by the reality of the history that was wrapped up in this racially motivated massacre. I was also overwhelmed because the proximity of this incident made it personal.

I know all about attending church in South Carolina on Wednesday evenings in June. Growing up in my home meant that Sundays were for worship, and Wednesday nights were for Bible study or hanging around church until Mom or Dad finished choir rehearsal. Summers were for Vacation Bible School. The churches I attended had dirt or gravel parking lots and small cemeteries off to the side, with tombstones surrounded by uncut grass, ant hills, and faded names above the birth and transition dates of those who had gone on before us. My childhood was filled with precious artifacts: old churches with pews, wooden floors, and chipped paint;

brick storefronts or white slab buildings with small crosses that showed passersby who we were, the legacy and history we held fast, and to whom we belonged. We belonged to Jesus.

So when Dylan Roof fired blazing hot rounds of bullets into those precious brown bodies, I know with certainty that it could have easily been me or one of my loved ones bleeding out on that church floor in South Carolina. By choosing this sacred place to carry out his murders, he came against the Creator, and he came against the truth about the identity of every black- and brown-skinned person. We too are made in the image of God, and therefore our lives have dignity and value. Our lives *and* our bodies matter.

While the Charleston shooting was a dark moment in our history, it was not an isolated incident. It is part of a long history of intentional violence and oppressive actions, which is perpetuated when "good people" turn a blind eye and do nothing.

With righteous action change is possible—but it's costly. For his resistance, Henry Smith was murdered. For demanding action, MLK was murdered. For her advocacy, Bree was arrested. The Orangeburg 3 and the Charleston 9 became martyrs, and their deaths were impetuses for change.

Dr. Brenda Salter McNeil calls experiences such as these catalytic events: "This term refers to the often painful but necessary experiences that happen to individuals and organizations and serve to jump-start the reconciliation process." She continues, "Most of us need this type of push to help us start the [reconciliation] journey. We need someone or something to push us out of our comfort zones and the isolated social enclaves that keep us alienated from other people and their differing perspectives." Such events have happened, and change has indeed occurred. Legal segregation is a thing of the past, we have made some progress concerning human rights, and the Confederate flag has been removed from the statehouse in South Carolina.

We all need to wake up! Knowing our history and facing tragedy make us more conscious people. Becoming conscious and demanding justice must not be the revolutionary acts of a select few in a society. Deep and lasting change will happen when we see the sacrificial and strategic actions of a unified body of justice seekers working together to demand it.

WHEN THE TIDE TURNS

When faced with this history, I am comforted by the truth of God's Word. The exodus narrative gives us the opportunity to read a biblical and historical story from the perspective of an oppressed people and their leader. Along with the call to consciousness in this account, we must not miss God's consistent presence on his people's journey out of Egypt and into the Promised Land. In reading, we learn the truth about the Israelites, and we also learn some fundamental truths about God.

God is omnipresent. As David reminds us, there is no place we can go to escape God's presence (Psalm 139:7-8). But more than God being everywhere, all the time, we might understand "that all things are present to God." We can rest in the knowledge that "there is nowhere in the universe that lies beyond the cognition (and care) of God." When my hope for a better future wanes, I stand on the truth that God is present throughout history, and he is also just. Paul has given these words of encouragement: "[God] will pay back trouble to those who trouble you and give relief to you who are troubled, and to us as well. This will happen when the Lord Jesus is revealed from heaven in blazing fire with his powerful angels" (2 Thessalonians 1:6-7). In spite of how things look today, know that God is just. When all is said and done, he will do what is right.

God is omniscient. He sees and knows all, and because of his consciousness, he will act. This is one of the truths of God's character that we learn from Moses' story. When God met Moses at the burning bush, he said,

> I have indeed seen the misery of my people in Egypt. I have heard them crying out because of their slave drivers, and I am concerned about their suffering. So I have come down to rescue them from the hand of the Egyptians and to bring them up out of that land into a good and spacious land, a land flowing with milk and honey. . . . The cry of the Israelites has reached me, and I have seen the way the Egyptians are oppressing them. So now, go. I am sending you to Pharaoh to bring my people the Israelites out of Egypt. (Exodus 3:7-10)

God called Moses because he saw the oppression of the Israelites, and the time had come to correct it.

God is also omnipotent, an attribute that reminds that God will overturn "evil for good." God will remain true and consistent to his own 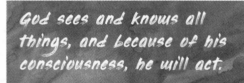 character. Paul's writing reminds us that the sin that appears to go unpunished or overlooked will most certainly be dealt with at the time of the Lord's judgment.

We learn throughout Scripture that God also often uses difficult circumstances to humble us and shape us into his likeness. In the physical realm, there is no doubt that Israel's enslavement lasted a long time. The slavery and injustices against black people in America have also lasted far too long. I don't have a sure answer for why God sometimes delays bringing about his justice.

Perhaps he is waiting for ordinary people like Moses who are willing to open their eyes to his presence and pay attention to how he instructs them to become his agents of change. When the

Israelites cried out to God, his response was, "I hear you, and I'm sending Moses." Someone has to take the risk of going to Pharaoh to demand that he let the people go. Someone has to break down doors when the invisible sign says "private" or "for members only." Someone has to organize a team, train them, and then execute the strategic plan so people can climb the flagpoles of domination and pull them down in the name of God.

Perhaps God wants to use this history to teach all of us that the suffering of this life humbles us, makes us more conscious people, and causes us to depend on God. This is a difficult biblical truth, and it is the reason we cry out to him when our hearts grow weary of the oppression and the burdens of this life (see Psalm 13:1-2).

Regardless of his sovereign reasons for delay, we know that God did bring both the Israelites and black people in America out of slavery, God did overturn Jim Crow, and God does and will implement righteous change on the earth. In his just time, God will do what is right because that is the very nature of his being. He is motivated to respond in this way.

On this life journey, we must be consciously aware and convicted that God hears, and he promises to answer the call of those who love him (Psalm 91:14-15). Sometimes his answer to the cries and needs of the people is *you*. We can respond to God's call to conscious action because we know that he will strengthen us for the work if our hearts are fully committed to him (2 Chronicles 16:9).

TRUTH IS: We must be aware of the history, artifacts, and stories that shape our lives before we can respond to God's call for justice.

REFLECTION QUESTION: What stories and history have significantly shaped your life, and how is God calling you to respond as a result?

SCRIPTURE MEDITATION:

Look on me and answer, L ORD my God.
Give light to my eyes, or I will sleep in death,
and my enemy will say, "I have overcome him,"
and my foes will rejoice when I fall.

But I trust in your unfailing love;
my heart rejoices in your salvation.
I will sing the L ORD 's praise,
for he has been good to me. (Psalm 13:3-6)

PERSONAL AFFIRMATION: God is good and just. He will certainly act, and sometimes that divine action is through me.

CALL TO ACTION: Have you taken time recently to look at the injustices in your local community? Consider going out of your way, taking a different route, or reading or watching a different news source this week. You don't have to agree with anything you read or hear, but do ask God: "What is being communicated? Why is it being communicated? Who is the target audience for the message? What am I feeling about the message? Why am I responding this way?"

PRAYER: Lord, I thank you for your faithfulness. In due time, you will act justly and make all things right in the world. Help me believe this truth and respond courageously in the meantime. Make me light where there is darkness. For your glory. Amen.

TWEET: God is aware and present to our suffering. He will act to implement righteous change in the earth. @asistasjourney #ASojournersTruth

CHAPTER SIX

DELIVERANCE

TRUTH IS, FREEDOM COMES TO THOSE WHO DEMAND IT

A "reverend" man, whose light should be
The guide of age and youth,
Brings to the shrine of Slavery
The sacrifice of truth!

FRANCES E. W. HARPER,
"BIBLE DEFENCE OF SLAVERY"

I would like to meet you." The email from a stranger arrived in my inbox without any warning. Because of the rarity of my maiden name, Sistrunk, the sender was able to find me while researching his family's history. He was curious about whether we might be related. I don't know the history of my last name, so I was intrigued. However, I was a vulnerable college student and my momma didn't raise no fool, so I didn't give him much information.

We exchanged emails, and I invited him to my upcoming US Naval Academy Gospel Choir concert. It was in a public space with high security, and I was surrounded by people who either loved me or had taken an oath to protect me. The odds were in my favor.

At the end of the concert we met in the lobby. He called out my name, and I approached a tall, heavy-set, white man who was old enough to be my father. We exchanged pleasantries; I thanked him for attending the evening's event. Then we parted and I never heard from him again.

When I first saw this man, my mind immediately went to the horrors of the slave plantation. He and I both knew the likelihood of where and how our stories might have intersected. It is common knowledge that Southern plantations were identified by the last name of the property holder and that those enslaved were given their master's last name. It is also known that slave owners frequently raped their female slaves, often producing offspring.

Given this history, I am not surprised that I never heard from him again. Perhaps he did not want to include me in his story. That's a typical response from white people who find themselves in a Thomas Jefferson and Sally Hemmings situation. When faced with these realities, we are all tempted to make the truth less horrific. Specifically, for people in the dominant group, the temptation is to remove themselves, claim colorblindness, insist that they are not racist, or otherwise ignore the issues. Regardless of how badly this stranger wanted to erase me or ignore this history, the truth still remains.

A NEGLECTED HISTORY

The truth is that we have always lived in a racialized society. Christian sociologists Michael O. Emerson and Christian Smith define a racialized society as one "wherein race matters profoundly for differences in life experiences, life opportunities, and social relationships." They add that such a society "allocates differential economic, political, social, and even psychological rewards to groups along racial lines; lines that are socially constructed."

I often use environmental pollution as a metaphor to discuss racism. Pollution, like racism, is a problem created by humans. All of us are negatively affected by it, and because it has been around for so long in our country it's easy to become comfortable with its existence. Some would even deny that global warming is real. We must consider the realities of both pollution and racism. Just because we don't always see or acknowledge the immediate side effects doesn't mean the problems don't exist, or that they are somehow going to autocorrect themselves.

The truth is, some people don't have the luxury or privilege of ignoring racism.

A daughter of slaves and an anti-lynching activist, Ida B. Wells proclaimed that "the way to right wrongs is to turn the light of truth upon them." Shining the light of truth helps us all walk in freedom. Shining the light of truth must become a consistent and intentional practice for all believers because without these moral checks, we re-create or continue to enforce the racial divisions and inequalities we claim to oppose. Unless we turn the light of truth on *all* of our history, we will continue as a morally corrupt nation. It is divisive to isolate certain parts of our shared story as "black history" without acknowledging how that history informs the lives, social structures, politics, and legacies of us all.

My strongest conviction toward advocacy is that God wants people to live freely. This conviction has put me on a path to pursue racial justice. As we consider this path, it's important to acknowledge that we are all on a continuum when it comes to crosscultural competence. Mark DeYmaz and Oneya Fennell Okuwobi, for example, describe a crosscultural continuum ranging from "cultural destructiveness" as one extreme to "cultural proficiency," which we aspire to. I don't expect significant movement on this spectrum from any person who doesn't claim to know Christ. Within the body of Christ, however, I do believe that we have a responsibility to educate ourselves about our history, to reject the status quo, to hold each other accountable to Christ's standards, and to work together to become a loving, united, and righteous people of God.

We must know our history or risk repeating it. Ignoring the past or remembering only selective parts does not make us a pious nation. On the contrary, it makes us all complicit in the sins and unjust structures that exist. Soong-Chan Rah takes this truth a step further when he writes:

> Our tendency to ignore our tainted history may arise from a warped self-perception. . . . An assumed exceptionalism belies the belief that we do not have to deal with our history because through our exceptional status we have overcome the past. The destruction of black bodies and black minds can be justified because their sacrifice helped to build our exceptional nation. Privilege and exceptionalism exempt us from engaging in the necessary work of dealing with our lamentable history.

The necessary work of dealing with this history includes rejecting the stereotypes and lies about people of color and agreeing that God desires all people to break free from these broken systems.

There are very practical ways to show you agree with these truths. If you hold a leadership position in the workplace, for example, you can require that qualified people of color are in the final candidate pool before you make a new hire, especially in the leadership echelons. Or you can ensure that people of color are receiving equal pay for their work. All of us can do a better job of researching, reading legislation, voting in every election, and contacting our political representatives to ask how marginalized people groups will be impacted by their policies.

Ignoring the past or remembering only selective parts does not make us a pious nation.

We can all educate ourselves. Seek out the stories of people of color by purchasing their books, reading their blogs, listening to their podcasts, or buying their magazines and art. Within the four walls of the church, you can interrogate theology and the ways you interpret Scripture by reading from the perspective of a suffering people group. Consider: What preachers are you listening to? What is the basis of their theology? Who is being quoted from the pulpit? What books are being discussed in small groups or Bible studies? Allow people of color to become your teachers.

The Israelites were so oppressed that they cried out to God. For centuries, black people have continued this spiritual practice of lament and praying for deliverance. Meditate on their words from this old Negro spiritual:

Go down, Moses, way down to Egypt land.
Tell old Pharaoh, let my people go.

God sent Moses from the slave house to the Egyptian palace with a prophetic message of deliverance. The centuries of slavery were over! We must continue to proclaim that prophetic message until all people are free from slavery in its various forms.

THEY DON'T WANT US TO TALK ABOUT SLAVERY

A brief look at the transatlantic slave trade reveals that more than ten million free Africans were stolen from their homeland and sold like cattle, then made to suffer cruel and unusual punishment, including torture, rape, and murder. This system was built on the social construct of race, which shaped a narrative of black inferiority. It allowed for generations of wealth building for white people in the South.

When the legal form of slavery finally ended, most freed slaves could not read or write. This lack of education meant that they didn't know what to do with money, even if they got their forty acres and a mule as compensation from the government.

It greatly troubles me that after the exodus from Egypt, God didn't completely abolish the system of slavery among the Israelites. He did, however, give all slaves the option of going free in their seventh year of work. He also said that they should never go away empty handed, as slave owners were required to liberally provide for their slaves at their departure (Deuteronomy 15:12-15). Black people have never received this level of compensation or reparation. African Americans started out as slaves—where they did not have free agency of their own minds, bodies, skills, work, resources, families, or property—and they left that system with nothing. These are historical facts we are too quick to forget.

Americans remember what we deem important. No one says to the Jewish community, "Get over the Holocaust and pretend it never happened." On the contrary, the United States Holocaust Memorial Museum was opened on April 26, 1986. But it was not until September 24, 2016, a full thirty years later, that the National Museum of African American History and Culture opened in our nation's capital. It is so easy for the dominant people group to call out injustices in other countries, while not taking a look at themselves to repent of the many ways they continue to terrorize people of color at home.

Go down, Moses, way down to Egypt land. Tell old Pharaoh, let my people go.

We must not forget that artifacts have meaning and depth. They send a clear message to the world about what we deem most important. I suppose those in the dominant people group want to avoid or ignore this conversation for numerous reasons. Our nation's heritage is embarrassing and can evoke feelings of guilt and shame. Quite frankly, others want to ignore this history and don't want us to talk about slavery because they don't want deliverance for the enslaved to ever come. Let's confess this truth and get to talking!

WHEN WILL DELIVERANCE COME?

The Israelites were God's chosen people. The Bible is very clear, however, that God did not choose Israel because they were righteous in any way. In fact, they were stubborn and rebellious against the Lord from the very beginning of the relationship (Deuteronomy 9:4-24). God delivered Israel and brought them into the Promised Land because of the wickedness of the nations living in the land (Deuteronomy 9:4-5), because of his desire to fulfill the covenantal promise he made to their ancestors (Deuteronomy 9:5), because of Moses' fervent prayers and intercession on behalf of the people (Deuteronomy 9:18-20; 10:10-11), and because of God's own righteousness and reputation (Deuteronomy 9:26-29).

God brought them out of slavery in spite of themselves. This biblical narrative is much more about God: his desire, his ability, and his willingness to directly engage his creation to bring about change on the earth. Can you perceive it? This biblical history speaks of the promise of freedom for anyone who cries out to God for help (see Exodus 2:23-24). Moses had a clear message for Pharaoh: The broken system of slavery will come to an end! According to God, slavery in all of its forms must cease!

What do you say about your country? Although we have seen progress in the United States, I've never believed that we lived in a post-racial society. I did consider that, with the changing racial demographics that will soon lead to whites being among the minority, we would eventually learn to respect each other's humanity, appreciate our differences, and work together for a better future.

That hope started to dwindle on July 13, 2013 when a jury acquitted George Zimmerman of the murder of seventeen-year-old Trayvon Martin. I was spending that Saturday evening in the home of my godparents, who were civil rights activists in their own right, and we were surrounded by the love and fellowship of our black friends. There were more than five generations among us, and we spent the day eating great food, laughing out loud, and reminiscing about the life, love, and legacy of our shared stories.

As the evening drew near a close, several of us migrated to the back porch, where the cool summer breeze kissed our faces. We watched the star lights twinkle on the surface of the river and cherished our cups of vanilla ice cream. It was a beautiful day. I glanced through the window into the kitchen, only to notice that several eyes were now glued to their cell phones. Before long, our tranquility had been disturbed and I heard the words, "The verdict is in."

We all moved quickly to gather around the main television in the family room. There we heard that George Zimmerman had been found not guilty on all counts. The message was clear: Trayvon's black life was not worthy of justice.

We sat in deafening silence for a few minutes. A black boy was dead, and his killer was now free. This is the refrain that keeps repeating itself. I fought back tears.

None of us knows exactly what happened in those final moments of Trayvon's life. We do know that he was walking through a neighborhood trying to get home. Besides his clothes and shoes, the only possessions on his black body were a cell phone, a bag of Skittles, and a bottle of sweet tea. We also know that if his killer, George Zimmerman, had simply followed the instructions of the 911 dispatcher, then Trayvon might have lived.

Incidentally, this murder happened in Florida, a "stand your ground" state. Did Trayvon have the right to stand his ground and fight for his own life? This case revealed again that there is often little grace in America for black people who insist on fighting for their freedom—who have the audacity to exercise their rights to life, liberty, and the pursuit of happiness. This endless assault on black lives with impunity finds its roots in the American soil of slavery. Slavery in all of its forms must cease!

Go down, Moses, way down to Egypt land. Tell old Pharaoh, let my people go.

Approximately one year later, events in the city of Ferguson became a real wake-up call for a new generation of black activists. For me, the awakening happened as riots and police brutality were documented live and reported through my Twitter newsfeed. The events on the ground were captured by the people who lived and were invested in Ferguson, by those who counted the cost of the devastating losses in their own community. My heart broke as I saw old black and white photos of police carrying assault rifles or siccing dogs on black people placed next to these new, colorful images of police in military assault gear and weapons patrolling the streets of Ferguson.

There have been far too many murders of innocent or unarmed black people to count. Some of them make national news or become hashtags, but others are known only to those immediately affected. In addition to the loss of their lives and the assaults on their characters, these victims have another thing in common: their killers continue to go free. From the first route of the transatlantic slave trade until now, the message in America has been that black lives do not matter.

STAND UP TO PHARAOH

When people of color cry out for justice, we are crying out to God for freedom. We do this for our own sake and for each other. It is also an opportunity for white people to see the error of a distorted message that has been perpetuated throughout history. It is a challenge to change the narrative and tell the truth. When the people of God collectively say, "black lives matter," it is a prophetic lament and cry for God to deliver, execute justice, and be a defense.

God sent the Israelites a savior. By the time Moses brought the message of deliverance to Pharaoh, the Israelites had been in Egypt for 430 years. "God heard their groaning and he remembered his covenant with Abraham, with Isaac and with Jacob. So God looked on the Israelites and was concerned about them" (Exodus 2:24-25). Because of his concern, God sent Moses to deliver a clear message to Pharaoh: "Let my people go."

Can you hear the cries of God's people throughout history?

Through blood and white supremacy. Let my people go.

Through frogs and slavery. Let my people go.

Through gnats and black codes. Let my people go.

Through flies and sharecropping. Let my people go.

Through the death of livestock and lynching. Let my people go.

Through boils and Jim Crow segregation. Let my people go.

Through hail and voter suppression. Let my people go.

Through locusts and racism. Let my people go.

Through darkness and the war on drugs. Let my people go.

Through death of your firstborn and mass incarceration. Let my people go!

Slavery in all of its forms must cease!

Go down, Moses, way down to Egypt land. Tell old Pharaoh, let my people go.

We must take the risk of having honest conversations. When people ask, "Why should Pharaoh let the Israelites go?" courageously tell them: because all humans are created in the image of God with dignity, inherent value, and the responsibility to exercise dominion on earth. No human has the right to lay hold of the lives of other humans; that power belongs to God alone. God charts the course of history, and he uses the lives of individuals to accomplish his highest good for all of his creation.

> All humans are created in the image of God with dignity, inherent value, and the responsibility to exercise dominion on earth.

THE HISTORY PHARAOH FORGOT

At the beginning of the exodus narrative, there is a statement that captures the historical context and the depth of systemic injustice Moses was born into: "Then a new king, to whom Joseph meant nothing, came to power in Egypt" (Exodus 1:8). It is easy to miss the significance of this statement, but there's a history lesson here. More than four hundred years prior to Moses' birth, there was an Israelite boy named Joseph. His jealous brothers sold him into slavery, and he was transported to Egypt. Joseph's integrity, work ethic, and gift of interpreting dreams eventually allowed him to become a trusted advisor to Pharaoh, the king of Egypt.

Because of Joseph, Pharaoh was able to maintain his wealth and sustain life as he knew it. And he was able to do this without fully embracing Joseph's identity.

We know this because when Joseph's biological family moved from Canaan to Egypt, they were assigned a plot of land in Goshen because they were shepherds and therefore abhorrent to the Egyptian people (Genesis 46:31-34). During the famine they got rations of food like everyone else, but they had limited ability to make decisions about their own life or welfare (Genesis 47:11-12). Joseph was the only one who was allowed free agency, and that was only because it benefited Pharaoh. Life was not the same for Joseph as for his biological family, although they came from the same people group.

In Joseph's story and in our society today, everyone is affected by the hardships of life and the systems-that-be in different ways. Is it possible to work beside someone and still not understand what their community is up against? We can grasp the disparities and respond appropriately only if we are in trusted relationships with people who are different from us, and if we incline our ears to hear the historical truth behind the personal stories. This is critically important work for those in the dominant people group. In 2013, a Public Religion Research Institute survey reported that the majority of white Americans do not have nonwhite friends, meaning they lack intimate relationships with nonwhite people they consider trustworthy or with whom they have important conversations. This dynamic makes it hard to get past false assumptions—including white people thinking they understand a different people group based on knowing only a few examples.

Perhaps this biblical narrative can help us all see how easy it is to make exceptions for a few upwardly mobile, minority-group members like Joseph while at the same time rejecting his full identity and the community from which he came. If the empire benefits, Joseph can survive while so many from his people group are confined to Goshen or left in Canaan to die. But if Joseph can actually rise and cause the salvation of many, how much more is possible when others like him are also given opportunities to thrive?

At the beginning of the exodus narrative, the new Pharaoh didn't know this history or wouldn't accept the contributions of Joseph. It's a myth that Pharaoh's nation became great all by itself! Joseph faithfully served the nation for eighty years, and that is how Pharaoh was able to take advantage of a bad situation and increase his own wealth.

Over four hundred years God also caused the Israelites to prosper and increase in numbers—in spite of their oppression—just as he'd said. The new Pharaoh's unfounded fear of their self-actualization, his loss of control, and the possibility of their rebellion is what caused him to enslave the Israelites (Exodus 1:9-11).

This is the historical context in which Moses delivered his prophetic message.

Go down, Moses, way down to Egypt land. Tell old Pharaoh, let my people go.

#BLACKLIVESMATTER

My mother would often say, "Right is right, and wrong is wrong." It is right to change the messages we deliver to the world about black people. "Black lives matter" is a prophetic message of freedom. When I say, "black lives matter," I am speaking about the truth that black people bear the *imago Dei*. *Imago Dei* is Latin for "image of God," and is rooted in Genesis 1:27 where God created humans and breathed his spirit to grant them the gift of life.

To be clear, I am not talking about the Black Lives Matter Movement. It is important to make this distinction because the movement consists of individuals and organizations that are doing justice work in which I am not involved, so I don't want to distort their contributions. I do, however, believe that we need to listen to the diverse voices that are crying out in the wilderness and carefully consider the solutions being offered by different groups.

As people who care about the fight for freedom and the pursuit of justice, we also need to seek out local or unknown leaders who desire to bridge the gaps between the younger and older generations; who acknowledge the importance of protesting in the streets while serving their communities in roles from laboring in the medical field to rocking corporate boardrooms; who pursue advocacy and education; and who create jobs and opportunity to ensure equity. Regardless of your skin color, age, or gender, we all can take some responsibility in this fight.

Like Jesus the great liberator, I long to offer a kingdom message that has spiritual and physical impact to bridge the perceived sacred and secular divides (see Luke 4:18-19). And more than forty years after she spoke them, I still agree with the words of civil rights activist Fannie Lou Hamer: "We've got to have some changes in this country, and not only changes for the black man, and only changes for the black woman, but the changes we have to have in this country are going to be for liberation of all people—because nobody's free until everybody's free."

What happens on the streets in our cities affects all of us. Whether or not women and ethnic minorities are at the table—or creating tables of their own—makes a significant difference for society's progress. The learning that does or does not take place in the classroom shapes generations. The jobs, businesses, and wealth ethnic minorities are able to obtain has a direct impact on the priorities of their philanthropic efforts. What happens at the voting booth and on Capitol Hill changes our lives. And whether the American church participates, isolates itself, or covers her ears will determine the weight of her influence.

We need a holistic gospel message that offers deliverance from the sins of racism and breaks the yokes of oppression that lead to death. This freedom cannot be denied. It must be demanded.

TRUTH IS: God offers a prophetic message that stands against the history and fears of the oppressor. We must proclaim God's message of freedom and actively pursue it.

REFLECTION QUESTION: What lies and historical messages have you believed about different people groups? How is God inviting you to change the narrative?

SCRIPTURE MEDITATION:
> From the LORD comes deliverance.
> May your blessings be on your people. (Psalm 3:8)

PERSONAL AFFIRMATION: "It is for freedom that Christ has set us free. Stand firm, then, and do not let yourselves be burdened again by a yoke of slavery" (Galatians 5:1).

CALL TO ACTION: Listen to artist Andra Day's song "Stand Up for Something" this week. Read the lyrics. Share it with a friend or two. How is God inviting you to stand up?

PRAYER: Deliver us, oh Lord. Up and out of slavery, deliver us. Up and out of oppression, deliver us. Up and out of generational bondage, deliver us. Up and out of the captivity of our own minds, deliver us, oh Lord. Make us walk in freedom. Amen.

TWEET: We need a clear gospel message that includes freedom from the sins of racism and breaks the yokes of oppression. @asistasjourney #ASojournersTruth

CHAPTER SEVEN

TRUST

TRUTH IS, WE HAVE A MONEY PROBLEM

God can handle the struggle of the deep; our
shallowness is what's really killing us.

LEROY BARBER, *EMBRACE: GOD'S RADICAL*
SHALOM FOR A DIVIDED WORLD

iddyup, Betsy."

"Betsy, giddyup."

"Giddyup, Betsy," my mom would say as she turned the ignition of her little blue car. This was one of my earliest childhood memories, living in our modest Orangeburg Manor apartment. Every morning my mother would plead with Betsy to do her job so that she would not be late for work and we would not be late for school. Eventually Betsy would start purring and we could ease on down the road, but we were always late.

By this time, my mother was divorced and it was just her, my little sister, and me. We were content, the three of us, and I didn't realize then how financially challenging things were because my mother kept a smile on her face. I didn't know that the cold cereal, the large silver can of peanut butter that sat on top of our refrigerator, the milk, the huge blocks of cheese, and the butter inside the fridge were all issued by the federal government. My mother worked full time, and yet we were on government assistance.

Eventually, my mom met and fell in love with Mr. William Johnson. They dated for a couple years and married when I was seven years old. My sister and I started calling him Dad right away. We weren't trying to erase my biological father—it's just that Mr. Johnson came into our lives and did what good fathers do. He was devoted to our family, and I was glad to have a father I could depend on.

LEARNING TO TRUST GOD AS FATHER

How is your relationship with your earthly father? I suspect that most people don't have a perfect relationship with their parents, but it is important to reflect on these relationships as they inform our views about God and our human need for connection and security. I didn't have a hard time trusting God as father because my own father was dependable. He was most certainly my protector. In him I had no doubt.

When Moses spoke to the Israelites about departing Egypt, they doubted. On several occasions after the exodus, they thought they had it better in Egypt and considered going back into slavery (Exodus 14:11-12; 16:3; Numbers 14:3-4). However, God persistently worked to grow their confidence in him. He told them again and again, "I am the Lord—put your trust in me."

I am the Lord who will bring you out of hardship and suffering.

I am the Lord who will free you from slavery and redeem your life.

I am the Lord who will make you my people, and I will be your God.

I am the Lord who keeps promises throughout generations (Exodus 6:6-8).

Whether we are slave or free, in Egypt or in the Promised Land, we must learn that God is the only one worthy of our trust. This God is known all across the world as a mother to the motherless and a father to the fatherless (Psalm 27:10; 68:5). The great deliverer will parent you! The Israelites declared boldly at the Red Sea,

The LORD is my strength and my defense;
   he has become my salvation.
He is my God, and I will praise him. (Exodus 15:2)

This was their boast right after they had doubted, and right after God destroyed their enemies in the Red Sea. This is my boast of the Lord today.

RED SEA MOMENTS

This trust and boasting in the Lord is not something that I learned from great victories. It is the song that plays in my heart whenever I have Red Sea moments—you know, those moments when we are tempted to become content in our old place of residence or when our future seems so uncertain and we don't know which way to go.

The seeds for learning to trust in God alone were not seeds of triumph; they were seeds of doubt. Although I was secure in my own home, entering college awakened me to the doubt that had taken root because I was disadvantaged economically.

At the Naval Academy, several of my white male classmates articulated how they had wanted to attend since they were children. Some of them were considered legacy kids because their families included alumni of the institution. Having a legacy provides access to affluent networks. I didn't know anything about such social connections; as a teenager I just wanted to graduate from college without debt. While I was focusing on graduation, several of my white classmates were already being invited, mentored, and sponsored into a new generation of wealth building.

> Whether we are slave or free, in Egypt or in the Promised Land, we must learn that God is the only one worthy of our trust.

In addition to lacking this social consciousness, I was also academically deficient, in spite of graduating at the top of my high school class and having a weighted GPA that exceeded 4.0. As an English major, I was embarrassed when my professors referenced authors, poets, and classics to which I'd had no previous exposure. I would shrink in my seat as classmates raised their hands to discuss material many of them had read several times, some as early as middle school. I'd always loved reading as a kid, and as a public school student I was always on the college-bound, honors, or Advanced Placement tracks. Why didn't anyone tell me what to read? Because I did not receive an academic preparation comparable to that of many of my classmates, I struggled academically all the way through college.

If reading about my disadvantages is moving you to wonder, *What can I do about any of these issues?* I say, commit to investing in the next generation. Don't take children on as special projects or charity cases that need fixing. Take them on as mentees who are worthy of your love and affirmation, tutor them as students who are capable of learning, and teach them how to read with comprehension and how to communicate through writing. Provide opportunities for them to learn, grow, and be challenged. Educate, expose, and prepare them for competitive entry into college and to receive scholarships.

Though I had come so far with support from my family and community, the new challenges of college felt like a sea that I was unsure how to cross.

WHEN TRUST GETS TESTED AT HOME

I was overwhelmed by the reality of what was normal for the majority of white kids who attend schools like the Naval Academy versus what was normal for most children who look like me. I had to come to grips with my own family history.

My dad was a roofing contractor by trade. He worked six days a week every week. I never saw him call in sick. Though both of my parents were working, money was always tight. The roofing business is steady work, but pay is inconsistent. My mother was anxious when my father worked and didn't get paid on time—and sometimes not at all. We were a part of the working poor.

In spite of their humble beginnings, my parents had a great partnership. Mom convinced Dad to start his own business. He acquired a business truck and a team of skilled workers, and our family wore blue "W. J. Roofing" hats and T-shirts with pride. Dad did the hard labor while Mom kept the books. We were doing all right for ourselves and slowly moved into the middle class.

I was not fully aware of how much my father taught me and how much I depended on him until the day he didn't show up for one of my track meets in the summer of 1992. When I heard "First call for the girls' one-hundred-meter hurdles!" I looked around, but there were no signs of him. I settled into the blocks and consoled myself that perhaps he was critiquing my race at a distance from somewhere around the field.

When I returned to the bleachers I learned that my family had been in a severe car accident. Dad had a few broken ribs, which led to three months of physical therapy, no chance of getting on a roof any time in the near future, and the loss of his employees and clientele. We went back to our lives, but all of us were fractured. This accident was the ruin of my father's small business and the resurfacing of our financial woes.

THE FINANCIAL DISPARITY OF BLACK AMERICANS

There was no margin, no safety net for us. This is a small part of my family's story, yet it is the historical reality of many hardworking black people. Stories are rarely told of those Americans who have worked an entire lifetime and are left with nothing to show for it. In his classic work *The Souls of Black Folk*, W. E. B. Du Bois wrote about the Negro who strived for upward mobility:

For the first time he sought to analyze the burden he bore upon his back, that dead-weight of social degradation partially masked behind a half-named Negro problem. He felt his poverty; without a cent, without a home, without land, tools, or savings, he had entered into competition with rich, landed, skilled neighbors. To be a poor man is hard, but to be a poor race in a land of dollars is the very bottom of hardships. He felt the weight of his ignorance,—not simply of letters, but of life, of business, of the humanities; the accumulated sloth and shirking and awkwardness of decades and centuries shackled his hands and feet.

In many ways, the lack of knowledge is a significant problem within the black community that perpetuates generational poverty. Historically, black families have acquired and maintained significantly less wealth than white families. The median wealth of white households was about ten times that of black households in 2016, according to the Pew Research Center. Pew also reported that "among full- and part-time workers in the U.S., blacks in 2015 earned just 75% as much as whites in median hourly earnings." In a study released in 2018, the Equality of Opportunity Project found that "black boys, even ones raised in wealthy families, living in the most well-to-do neighborhoods have always earned less than their white counterparts in adulthood." Because of the historical context, black families are without a safety net, so when any calamity strikes, it is fatal.

My family never recovered from the accident. More importantly, in only three months I witnessed the psychological and physical shattering of my father's hopes and dreams. It's a sad reality when you take what feels like your one chance for upward mobility, only to watch it crumble before your eyes. That leads to despair.

In his brilliant essay "The Case for Reparations," author Ta-Nehisi Coates quotes from a 1965 speech by President Lyndon B. Johnson:

> Negro poverty is not white poverty. Many of its causes and many of its cures are the same. But there are differences— deep, corrosive, obstinate differences—radiating painful roots into the community, and into the family, and the nature of the individual.
>
> These differences are not racial differences. They are solely and simply the consequence of ancient brutality, past injustice, and present prejudice.

The president was speaking to my father's generation, but this history continues to affect all generations.

I knew my family was struggling financially, but I didn't realize how much until my mother died. A little more than six years after the car accident and family crisis, she was gone. Having suffered years of ailments in her heart and kidneys, her physical body gave out. My mother had her first major surgery to fix a heart aneurysm in her early thirties. Her death in December 1999 was the result of a second heart surgery. She had no life insurance (not for lack of trying, but because of her preexisting health conditions—and we simply couldn't afford it). Because our family lacked the money, her body lay in the hospital room for two days until some friends called to pay the funeral home to come and properly lay her to rest.

Coates reminds us, "The wealth gap merely puts a number on something we feel but cannot say—that American prosperity was ill-gotten and selective in its distribution. What is needed is the airing of family secrets, a settling with old ghosts." What's your family's story? My nasty, dirty little family secret is that we were poor.

The thought that I was unable—as a loving daughter and oldest child, and as a midshipman without a real paying job—to help my deceased mother haunts me like a ghost. When she died, I again felt small, embarrassed, inadequate, and helpless. That's a lot of emotion to pile on top of grief. At twenty years old I didn't know what to do with it; I only knew that I didn't ever want to feel that way again.

FINANCIAL ASSURANCE

All of these seeds of doubt and lack of preparation were planted deep down in my heart, and I desperately wanted something different. I didn't want to accumulate wealth because I was materialistic. I just had a profound sense deep in my soul that I could be of better service to myself, my family, and others if I had money to spare.

I paid attention to God's desire to provide for his own people in the Old Testament (see Deuteronomy 28:9-13). Those promises are echoed in the New Testament; the apostle Paul understood that financial blessings from God could result in generosity and equity among believers (2 Corinthians 8:10-15; 9:6-15). Is this the way you view the purpose of money? We cannot talk about the historical effects of economic disparity without checking our own views regarding money—who has it, who doesn't, and why. Then, what just action is God calling us to when we get it?

Have you thought about financially supporting businesses, nonprofits, and schools that are owned or operated by people of color? Or perhaps you can offer financial literary education for uninformed communities. Maybe you feel called to tutor a student who needs some extra attention. People

> We cannot talk about the historical effects of economic disparity without checking our own views regarding money.

cannot give what they do not have. They cannot sell possessions they do not own (see Acts 2:44-45; 4:32-37). When people are given the opportunity to become educated and thrive economically, it results in an increase of generational wealth and their generosity going back into communities in need (without perpetuating a false narrative or attaching strings).

THE UNCERTAINTIES OF LIFE

I liked the financial benefits of graduating from the Naval Academy. Within a few short years, I was earning a six-figure salary. The passing of time also brings a change in priorities. Two years after graduation, I was married; three years after that, we had our baby girl, and our country was at war. I was faced with a dilemma as to whether I would continue my career in the military.

I loved being a US Marine and my work as a financial management officer. I loved the people I worked with and the community we built together. I liked the income. I loved my one-year-old daughter. But I had been close enough to the reality to know that I did *not* love the idea of going to war. Additionally, our marriage was in trouble, so we needed to work on that.

As I wrestled with God—being honest about my uncertainties and naming all of the things I loved and did not want to give up—his message to me became clear. God's question for my heart was, Do you trust me to provide for you, or do you trust the military to provide? I decided to trust God alone, and I gave up my career in the military.

Next came a new and exciting opportunity to work at the Department of Homeland Security (DHS). Taking this position was a slight decrease in pay, but we were still doing quite well financially. This transition was another test—an uprooting of all those seeds I had been watering in my heart and allowing to grow for so many years. Trusting God was a test I thought I'd passed, until I realized that more roots needed pulling. In fact, the whole soil needed tilling.

Although I was grateful to work at DHS, it didn't feel like a permanent career move. My priorities were still changing. After work, I was often leading small groups and Bible studies out of our home. Teaching the Word of God became a passion that I wanted to take seriously, so I applied to seminary. Then God started waking me up in the middle of the night to write. I had every intention of maintaining the status quo—writing as a side hustle and working my way through seminary. But then my husband lost his job in Maryland and landed a new one in North Carolina.

We had purchased our first home in Glen Burnie, Maryland—a brand-new house with a fenced-in yard in an old and rundown neighborhood—from a fast-talking developer and with the encouragement of a less-than-engaged real estate agent. This was before HGTV became the phenomenon that it is today, and before I knew anything about curb appeal, down payments, equity, or property value. If we had had more financial literacy, we would have rented instead. Our ignorance was evident when we attempted to sell the house, which we'd purchased during the housing peak of 2005–2006 with a subprime loan and no down payment. We became victims of the housing bubble. I hate to think of myself as a victim, but that is exactly what you become when you lack knowledge about a situation.

We spent more than a year trying to sell or rent the property, so for a year I drove back and forth between North Carolina and Washington, DC, for work. After all of our savings had been depleted, the house still did not sell.

Devastated, I quit my job at DHS so I could be home with my family and focus on seminary studies. Pull roots. Till soil. I wrestled with this decision for over a year. Again, it felt like I was giving up everything, but God's question for my heart was the same: Do you trust me to provide for you, or do you trust the government to provide?

For many years, God has been teaching me to trust him alone. This was also a fundamental lesson God taught the Israelites: do not put your trust in Pharaoh, the government, and its systems. We cannot put our trust in houses or cars or land. We cannot put our trust in jobs or money. I know now that I can't even trust the motivations or intentions of my own heart without God's Word and wise counsel.

THE GREAT I AM

Throughout the exodus narrative, God is teaching everyone a simple truth: he is God alone, and nothing else is worthy of worship. God speaks this truth against the false narrative that because of Pharaoh's earthly power structures he is a god worthy of worship. He speaks this truth against the false narrative that the Israelites desire to worship God because they are weak and lazy (Exodus 5:8).

Once God speaks the truth, the Israelites have an opportunity to reject all the lies and give up their dependency on Egypt. They learn that sometimes things get worse before they can get better. We learn from them that we must change our minds about earthly things, even our accumulation of money and wealth, if we are to follow God wholeheartedly.

Trust in God alone. Governmental authorities are set up by him to establish human society and build healthy communities (Romans 13:1-7). They are not worthy of our worship, and they cannot justify the abuse of power, the perpetuation of a widening wealth gap, or the enslavement of souls. If God is God, then Pharaoh is not. If God is God, then Caesar is not. If God is God, then the president of the United States is not, the government is not, the military is not, and the legal system is not. He is God alone!

God told Moses to tell the people truth about the great I Am. The problem with Pharaoh and Egypt is they think they have more power than they actually do, and the problem with us is that too often we believe them. I believed that getting a good education, a good job, and a good income would provide me with a sense of security. Nothing is wrong with having those things. It's just that I, like so many of us, have been taught to put my trust in them.

God knows better. God can tell the real from the fake. God knows what is imitation, deception, or demonic activity. The Egyptian magicians repeatedly tried to copy the miraculous signs done through Moses and Aaron, but God proved to all the Egyptians that he was the true God. He would not stand for trickery with Pharaoh and the Israelites, and he will not stand for false worship to grow in us. He required that Pharaoh let his people go so they could worship him alone, in the right way (Exodus 8:1, 20; 9:1, 13; 10:3).

We were created to worship the Creator, not his creation. If we worship God alone, then there is no place in our hearts to worship our pedigree, legacy, career, or income. Often God allows the hardships and plagues in our lives so that we "may know there is no one like the LORD our God" in all the earth (Exodus 8:10; see also 9:14, 29). We must trust in God alone.

TRUTH IS: We are tempted to put our trust in a lot of earthly things, but our only real assurance is in God.

REFLECTION QUESTION: What are the ways and areas in which God is inviting you to place your trust in him?

SCRIPTURE MEDITATION:

> I am the LORD, and there is no other;
>   apart from me there is no God. (Isaiah 45:5)

PERSONAL AFFIRMATION: You are God alone. In you I place my trust.

CALL TO ACTION: Take time this week for personal reflection in the presence of God. Consider journaling a response to these questions: How do I define success? Why do I define success in this way? What will I do once I have reached my definition of success? Then take a look at your budget (Step 1: Do you have a budget?) and pray about the ways you have managed the money God has entrusted to your care. Might God be inviting you to adjust your priorities?

PRAYER: You are God all by yourself. You are mother and father to me. You are my strength and my defense in times of trouble. You are my salvation, my provision, my hope. I belong to you. I will praise your name forever because you alone are worthy of praise. I will exalt you, Most Holy One. Amen.

TWEET: We are tempted to put our trust in a lot of earthly things, but our only real assurance is in God alone. @asistasjourney #ASojournersTruth

PART THREE

WILDERNESS

A voice of one calling:
"In the wilderness prepare
the way for the Lord;
make straight in the desert
a highway for our God. . . .
And the glory of the LORD will be revealed,
and all people will see it together.
For the mouth of the LORD has spoken."

ISAIAH 40:3, 5

We now make the treacherous journey of a sojourn into the wilderness. It is the place where we exchange the bondage of slavery for hope of the Promised Land. We shed the old and put on the new.

In the wilderness, we become trapped in an ugly place—where our emotions bubble to the surface and our senses reek with the blood of black and brown bodies crying out from the ground. Get angry. Lament. Shed hot tears. Pray. Look for inspiration wherever you can find it. Tell stories. Listen, and then ponder: "Where is our hope even in the midst of suffering and death? Does our understanding of a historical reality impact our current reality?"

Now is the time for humble reflection and decision. The wilderness brings both death and life. In the wilderness we learn to seek justice, to fight for that blessed hope. We find that we are spiritually destitute. We learn to live differently, because if we can't find ways to truly live, then we are dead after all.

CHAPTER EIGHT

ANGER

**TRUTH IS, THERE'S SOMETHING
THAT CAN KILL YOU**

*Anger has a long history of bringing
about positive change.*

CHIMAMANDA NGOZI ADICHIE,
WE SHOULD ALL BE FEMINISTS

*I*t was a last-minute decision to go on the retreat with the women from my church. I had spent quite a bit of time working and traveling that year, and I was expending more money on ministry than I was making. I was tired and just wanted to be home wrapped in my favorite blanket on the living room couch, where I could binge watch a few mindless shows for the weekend. However, someone thought I needed a different kind of rest, so they made it possible for me to attend the retreat. And I went.

I was asked to participate in the karaoke show, so I threw a cocktail dress in my bag, along with a few wigs (because I like having options). On the first night of the retreat, I put on my dress, heels, and a wig, and then—lights, camera, action—I sashayed onto the platform. Before beginning a lip sync of Aretha Franklin's song "Respect," I gave the women a brief exaltation based on Ephesians 5.

"People are always talking about how men need respect, and women desire good loving. We all know that men are from Mars and women are from Venus. In some ways, we have different needs, but I'm here to tell ya, to truly be loved is to also be respected. Can women get some respect too?"

I stared right into the eyes of the one man who was in the room, working the AV equipment (poor guy). All the women roared with laughter.

I gladly joined in, knowing all the while there was quite a bit of truth behind my words. Having grown up in a strict household, served in the U.S. Marine Corps, spent the majority of my professional career in male-dominated work spaces, and lived in a society where the injustices of racism and sexism are prevalent, I know disrespect is no laughing matter. My worst days consist of me yelling at my daughter because she did not obey on the third or fifth time. Her disobedience feels like disrespect to me, and I don't take too kindly to it from anybody. Being disrespected makes me angry.

AN ANGRY MAN

Moses was an angry man. His anger caused him to kill someone, to stand up for justice, and to miss the Promised Land. Anger is not all bad; the Bible instructs us, "In your anger do not sin" (Ephesians 4:26). We can get angry because God gets angry. Anger alone is not the problem, but what we do with that anger can be dangerous.

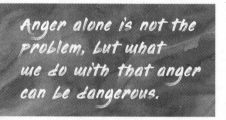

Anger alone is not the problem, but what we do with that anger can be dangerous.

We first notice Moses' anger streak when he sees an Egyptian physically beating one of his own people, a Hebrew slave. This injustice moved Moses to kill the Egyptian and hide his body in the sand (Exodus 2:11-14). Because of this violent act, he was forced to flee to Midian.

When he arrived in Midian, his first human encounter was at a well. There he observed shepherds taunting girls who were attempting to draw water. The narrative leads us to believe that this was a regular occurrence that often delayed the sisters' return home (Exodus 2:15-21). When Moses saw the shepherds' behavior, he had a "Not today, Satan!" attitude. He came to the girls' aid. There were multiple shepherds and only one Moses, and he was a stranger in a foreign land. I don't think he asked them nicely.

When Moses went to deliver the "Let my people go" message to Pharaoh, I think he was initially hopeful for a logical negotiation— even though God had informed him that Pharaoh wouldn't listen. Moses asked, reasoned, pleaded, prayed, but Pharaoh's heart was hard. When the time came for Moses to declare the final plague— death of the first born—he was "hot with anger" because Pharaoh refused to obey the Lord (Exodus 11:8).

When the Israelites finally left Egypt, Moses' anger turned toward his own people because they were constantly grumbling and complaining against God. They would not obey even his smallest instruction, such as "Keep no manna until morning" (Exodus 16:19-20). God wanted them to trust him to provide their daily bread, but some refused to listen.

The Israelites were a stubborn and thankless group, so God himself regularly became angry with them. They were impatient with God and even created a golden calf to worship. At this act of disobedience, God said to Moses, "Leave me alone that my anger may burn against them and that I may destroy them. Then I will make you into a great nation" (Exodus 32:10). The holy God has a right to get angry at sin, and he has the right to respond how he chooses to acts of disobedience.

Because of Moses' love and compassion for his own people, however, he passed on God's offer. Instead he interceded on their behalf. He pleaded with God, "Turn from your fierce anger; relent and do not bring disaster on your people" (Exodus 32:12). Because of Moses' prayers, God withheld judgment.

However, when Moses came face-to-face with the reality and gravity of the people's sin, his heart burned with anger. He broke the first tablets of the Ten Commandments, he ground the golden calf into powder, and he made the Israelites drink it! He then called all of the faithful servants of the Lord to join him in cleansing the Israelite camp. The Levites went out and killed everyone who had rejected the Lord. In the Old Testament law, the consequence for willful disobedience was always death, and God saw this killing as a righteous act of his judgment. On that day three thousand Israelites fell by the sword (Exodus 32:19-29).

In spite of the consequences of their blatant disregard for God, the Israelites continued to complain and rebel. There was no water as they journeyed through the wilderness of Zin, so Moses and Aaron asked the Lord to provide (Numbers 20:1-13). God gave them specific instructions to command a rock, trusting that the rock would obey its Creator and yield water for them to drink. But Moses was angry with the rebellious people, so he struck the rock instead. The water did come, "but the LORD said to Moses and Aaron, 'Because you did not trust in me enough to honor me as holy in the sight of the Israelites, you will not bring this community into the land I give them'" (Numbers 20:12). And just like that, Moses' anger caused him to miss the Promised Land.

ANGER AND INJUSTICE

I don't want to live in anger. I am aware of "the angry black woman" stereotype and have tried to reject it by swallowing my anger, relying on my faith, forgiving, turning the other cheek, and intentionally pursing diverse relationships. God requires this of me if I am to truly love my neighbor. After almost a decade of submitting to this spiritual work, I have found myself hurt by the reality that I have actively tried to love those who simply do not care about people who look like me—even in the church. This makes me angry.

I am angry that there is no place of safety for black people in America. I am angry that far too many black and poor children don't get to live up to their full potential because of systemic injustices and a public school system that so often fails them. I'm angry that their parents sometimes lack the education, support, and social structures needed to help their children thrive. I'm angry about slavery (past and present). I'm angry that women are marginalized and not paid fairly for their work. I'm angry that the American church is oftentimes too slow and too passive about almost everything that matters. I'm angry that people have to fight for basic rights like clean water, healthy food, safe shelter, and health care. I'm angry when people abuse children. I'm angry every time a black person gets shot by the state with impunity. I'm angry when lies, myths, and alternative facts are perceived as truth because folks don't read, have compassion for, or initiate relationships with people who are different from them, or simply don't care enough to check a source. I'm angry about a lot of things.

Columbia Business School professor Hitendra Wadhwa writes, "Great leaders often have a strong capacity to experience anger. It wakes them up and makes them pay attention to what is wrong in their environment, or in themselves. Without anger, they would not have the awareness or the drive to fix what is wrong." What makes you angry? If there is no anger, then perhaps there is no consciousness.

When we are angry about the things that make God angry, that is a righteous, not a self-centered, anger. Moses was angry about all of the right things: slavery, injustice, abuse of power, mistreatment of women, and his own people's disobedience toward God. Once we are awakened to injustices, it's time to put this righteous anger to good use.

The question the faithful servant of God must face is: What do we do with the anger that so deeply plagues us? For years I have been wrestling with God about the right actions to take in the face of so much injustice. Do I write? Do I protest? Do I leave or stick with a ministry, relationship, or community? Do I withhold funds? Do I speak up? Do I lobby or advocate? Do I vote or educate? Do I use social media? Do I lead or submit to local grassroots efforts?

> Once we are awakened to injustices, it's time to put this righteous anger to good use.

Our responses to injustice and anger may vary from day to day, but one thing is for sure: we don't have the option of doing nothing. The first righteous step is repenting for our part in injustice, and then we work toward righteous action. At a conference I once had the privilege of sitting at the feet of civil rights activist Rev. Dr. C. T. Vivian. When discussing action and advocacy he said, "It is in the action we find out who we are." If we don't take action in the face of injustice, we prove ourselves to be cowards. We must act!

VIOLENT ACTION

When God sent the Israelites into the Promised Land, he was taking just action against an abominable people (Genesis 15:12-19). Because the people in the land were idolatrous and worshiped pagan gods, God called for their total destruction (Deuteronomy 12:2-3; 13:1-18). The penalty for treason against God was death (Deuteronomy 13:5). This punishment was carried out at the hands of the Israelites, and God promised to show them compassion and to bless them for their obedience (Deuteronomy 13:17-18). There are periods throughout the Bible where God exercises his righteous anger in violence.

We see God working through violence even in the New Testament. When Jesus went to the cross, he was fighting for us through submitting to the violent act of crucifixion. Professor

Richard A. Horsley writes, "The Romans deliberately used crucifixion as an excruciatingly painful form of execution by torture (basically suffocation), to be used primarily on upstart slaves and rebellious provincials. It was usually accompanied by other forms of torture, such as severe beatings." People who are drawn only to the love, grace, and peace of Jesus do not know him fully and cannot rightfully understand him without acknowledging the physical violence and brutality of his death. We cannot ignore that it was God the Father's will to crush his Son with pain (Isaiah 53:10). Because of the Father's righteous anger toward sin, Jesus' death was required. This was a human death suffered by God's divine Son, and while the paradox of how God's eternal Son could die as a human being is tantalizing, the point here is that death—even a violent death—was necessary to set us free from sin.

It was not until I attended the Duke Divinity School Summer Reconciliation Institute in 2015 that I was given permission to publicly ask, "Is God violent?" A Christian grassroots organizer, Jamye Wooten, posed this question. He is a black father of a black child who lives in Baltimore, Maryland. His eyes watered as he showed us a picture of his teenage daughter protesting the acquittal of police officers associated with the death of Freddie Gray. His daughter was prepared to act!

After eloquently outlining a history of violence that the United States has imposed on black and brown citizens, as well as the violence our government has imposed on vulnerable countries all across the world, Wooten asked questions about the public expression of pain by different groups: "Do blacks or the most marginalized in our society have the right to express frustration, anger, and outrage? Do they have the right, even, to be violent?"

In his book *Let Justice Roll Down*, John M. Perkins writes, "Violence is a reaction of whites to black people who want nothing more than their freedom. . . . The worst violence is the violence against blacks. That is the violence—violence that usually is accepted so nicely within the white system that it gets no publicity at all." When considering American history, we must look at all of the black bodies fallen at the hands of white oppression, as Jamye Wooten urged in his talk.

Wooten wasn't advocating violence. He was simply stating the facts in the face of common white narratives that negatively portray people like Nat Turner or Malcolm X, or white analysis of organizations like the Black Panther Party or the Black Lives Matter Movement. Americans in the dominant group refuse to acknowledge that "people tend to resort to acts of terrorism only when previously available channels of communication have been closed off and other forms of protest have proved ineffective or futile." I believe Wooten was asking us to seriously ponder this question: Are blacks the only people in America who are not allowed to be violent in a system that continues to violently oppress them?

In his article "Who Has the Right to Be Violent?" Wooten writes that "America was founded on violence, and I suppose it will continue to be violent." He then invites readers to consider these questions:

> Is there a moral response to state-sponsored terror beyond nonviolent civil disobedience? Is violence only an option for the powerful, white, and Christian?
>
> Who gets to decide when violence is acceptable, moral, and even Christian? Who gets to decide that a brick [thrown] in Baltimore is more violent than . . . a police officer's gun in Louisiana, or, for that matter, a drone in Pakistan?

As people of faith, we cannot continue to have spiritual conversations and sermons that ignore the historical and persistent realities of violence. We cannot deny that violence has a place in

Scripture. But it is God alone who determines what is just, and he ultimately works for the redemption of his creation and for the rescue of the oppressed.

God promised Moses and the Israelites a land. To fulfill this promise, he used them to exercise his righteous judgment on people groups that had rejected him for over four hundred years. Centuries later, God used unjust people groups to exercise judgment on his own people, the Israelites, for their disobedience. Soong-Chan Rah reminds us that God does not show partiality in his judgments. He writes, "If God stays true to his character, he has to judge unrighteousness and injustice because he takes sin seriously. And because God is faithful to bring judgment upon Israel's disobedience, there is also certainty to God's redemption." God will judge, and he will also redeem.

WHEN ANGER GETS DANGEROUS

It is not beyond my human will to kill. That's a frightening confession, I know, but we must be honest with ourselves and others. That's why I don't advocate violence—its only satisfaction is death, and death is an enemy of us all.

From the first day I entered military training, I was disciplined by a Marine Corps gunnery sergeant. He was the one who taught us military drill, inspected our rooms, and prepared us for physical and combat training. We laced up our boots, grabbed our rifles, and daily marched to cadences like this one:

> The engines are running, we're ready to go
> We'll kill the enemy and steal their souls
> So early, so early, so early in the mornin'.

Turn a human into an enemy—that's how easy it is to prepare for and welcome death. It's hard to kill a human; it's much easier to murder an enemy.

Jesus did not use Morse code when he leveled the ground regarding anger and murder (Matthew 5:21-22), and he was not using classified files when he instructed, "Love your enemies and pray for those who persecute you" (Matthew 5:44). In the greatest sermon ever given, he was very clear about his Commander's intent.

If history has taught us anything, it most certainly has revealed that hating makes it easy to murder. That's why I choose love over hate. On the other hand, we must acknowledge the danger that exists when systems are built to support the thriving of one people group at the expense of other people groups, especially when those systems are perpetuated by violence. I find it gravely unjust to critique only the violent responses of black people without first analyzing the systems that provide cause for such responses in the first place. Redemption comes only when godly judgment is executed without partiality in the face of sin.

God himself provided deliverance for Israel when they were pursued by a violent enemy. The same God is active and present today. Do you believe it? Then go and proclaim the truth! Stand with the people and watch the deliverance of the Lord. Remind them that God fights for us; we need only to remain still (Exodus 14:13-14)—not inactive but assured that God will indeed act.

Someone has to raise the staff to part the Red Sea and tell an uncertain people, with troubled waters in front of them and a great army behind, to walk right on through. The angry waters and the angry army will not destroy you!

TRUTH IS: Anger is an appropriate response to sin because sin makes God angry. The wrestling within our souls is what to do with our righteous anger.

REFLECTION QUESTION: What is the proper place for my anger? How can I respond in anger and not sin against the Lord or other people?

SCRIPTURE MEDITATION:

> Be still, and know that I am God;
>> I will be exalted among the nations,
>> I will be exalted in the earth. (Psalm 46:10)

PERSONAL AFFIRMATION: I am not a coward. In the face of injustice, I must take the risk to act.

CALL TO ACTION: Name one injustice that makes you angry. How can you educate yourself about that one thing and consistently take righteous action?

PRAYER: God, I know that you are patient with us in our afflictions of the heart. When you get angry, you respond with justice. Help me to trust you in the face of every adversity, when death is all around, and when your timing does not seem perfect. Help me to trust your ability to war on my behalf and tear down the walls of injustice. In Jesus' name, amen.

TWEET: It's hard to kill a human; it's much easier to murder an enemy. @asistasjourney #ASojournersTruth

 DEATH

TRUTH IS, REMEMBERING CAN BRING US TOGETHER

But death is a slave's freedom.
We seek the freedom of free men.

NIKKI GIOVANNI, "THE FUNERAL OF
MARTIN LUTHER KING, JR."

When I told people that I was going to Rwanda, the immediate response was often "Be safe"—as if brown bodies are any less safe in Africa than they are in America. In the weeks leading up to that trip, I was speaking to someone about this book. When I finished sharing, she said, "Now God is leading you into the wilderness." I paused momentarily because I had several thoughts and emotions as I prepared for the trip, but I did not think for a moment that I was going into the wilderness. It isn't surprising that this came to her mind, however. Since the 1994 Rwandan genocide, danger is often the first idea the country's name invokes.

REMEMBERING IN RWANDA

I first learned about the genocide through Rwandan survivor Immaculée Ilibagiza's bestselling memoir, *Left to Tell.* With the release of the movie *Hotel Rwanda* I was again reminded of its brutality.

However, it wasn't until I read Gary Haugen's book *The Locust Effect: Why the End of Poverty Requires the End of Violence* that this feeling of horror again enveloped my heart. His vivid description of the genocide where "nearly a million people had been slaughtered—mostly by machete—in a span of about 10 weeks" brought the atrocity into horrifying focus by displaying the impact on an entire people group.

During his investigation as director of the UN Special Investigations Unit in Rwanda, Haugen ended up in a town south of Kigali, Ntarama, "in a small church compound where all the bodies remained just as their killers had left them—strewn wall to wall in a knee-high mass of corpses, rotting clothes, and the desperate personal effects of very poor people." He writes of the scene:

> The forensic experts were . . . picking through the remains and lifting out each skull for a simple accounting: "Woman—machete. Woman—machete. Child—machete. Woman—machete. Child—machete. Child—blunt trauma. Man—machete. Woman—machete . . ." On and on it went for hours.

He concluded, "What was so clear to me was the way these very impoverished Rwandans at their point of most desperate need, huddled against those advancing machetes in that church, did not need someone to bring them a sermon, or food, or a doctor, or a teacher, or a micro-loan. They needed someone to restrain the hand with the machete—and nothing else would do."

Who is going to restrain the hand with the machete? That was the question of justice in Rwanda.

When I read Haugen's book, I didn't know that I would find myself in the wilderness at that same church—now a genocide memorial—only three years later. I witnessed the shrapnel marks on the ceiling and floor where terrorists had tried to enter the church. I saw how they broke in through the gates of the sanctuary. I listened as the tour guide informed us that the terrorists were trained by and received weapons from the French government. They were taught how to kill quickly and effectively, and machetes were their weapons of choice because bullets were too expensive. I looked at the rotted clothes that still remain in the pews, the broken statue of Mary still attached to the wall, and the crutches of the disabled still resting on the table where congregants most likely took Communion on brighter days. I walked through that sanctuary of death and into an all-white room.

Centered in the room was a display case filled with cracked skulls and bones of different shapes and sizes, reminding us that real people had suffered horrendous deaths. Below them lay the casket of a girl who was raped and run through with a pole before she was brutally murdered. Her skeleton used to be on open display, but gazing at her remains caused survivors too much trauma, so they laid her bones to rest in a white casket marked with a brown wooden cross.

We came out of the darkness of that sanctuary and walked into the glorious Rwandan sunlight. Our tour guide escorted us with the etiquette of a mortician down into the mass graveyard. Death was all around me. I watched the guide's mouth move, but numbness blocked my hearing. She lifted the tops of caskets to reveal more skulls and bones, and I looked away.

The Nyamata Genocide Memorial is one of approximately one hundred genocide memorials located throughout Rwanda. The credo "Never Again, Never Forget" is on display at several of these public sights. Rwandans want people to see the horror of their history, and they want us all to remember.

What I learned in Rwanda is that if a nation truly wants to welcome redemption, then her citizens must first choose to acknowledge all the unjust deaths. We must remember the names and stories of those captured, enslaved, raped, lynched, oppressed, beaten, and unlawfully jailed. We are all connected. We can invite their stories to become a part of our stories, not because we want to live in the past or feel shame or guilt, but because remembering honors their humanity and just might remind us of our own.

Brené Brown writes, "Owning our stories is standing in our truth. It's transformative in our personal and professional lives AND it's also critical in our community lives. . . . Until we find a way to own our collective stories around racism in [the United States], our history and the stories of pain will own us." Because they remember and tell the truth, Rwandans are not owned or defined by the single narrative of the history of genocide in their country. Their redemptive story will be defined by how they continually come together and rebuild in light of that history.

Memorials hold the artifacts and the stories that help us remember.

LEARNING HOW TO RECONCILE

Surveying the history I've shared in this book reminds me that Americans are a prideful people. Unless there is clear monetary gain, learning from another country that does things differently—even when there is clear evidence of success—is a foreign concept. Today Rwandans are living as a reconciled people, and for that reason alone they have much to teach us.

I went to Rwanda not as a missionary but as a learner, and I watched the Christian ministry Africa New Life play a significant role in the country's transformation. The ministry is modeling a new way ahead by bringing rich kids and poor kids from diverse backgrounds together for worship, community, and education. There are no sacred-secular divides regarding their work, which incorporates the fields of health care, education, vocational training, and community development.

Whenever Africa New Life builds a school, they also build a church so they can join God in his transformation of hearts and minds. Rwandan children know their country's troubled history and how it has impacted every family and neighbor. When they are brought together from different tribes and economic classes to learn and live in boarding school, a mutual respect and understanding grows. They become adults who consciously lead and partner to pursue a redemptive mission for their country. The ways we choose to educate can unify and help us remember.

Remembering and rightly responding has caused Rwandan citizens to get involved in the justice system through the *gacaca* courts. These courts bring together survivors, perpetrators, and witnesses before locally chosen judges to prosecute genocide and other crimes against humanity. *Gacaca* courts use a restorative and retributive justice approach based on the basic human need for truth telling and the goal of ending a culture of impunity. The majority of Rwandans believe that confession is essential for reconciliation, that this process has brought unity between different tribes and improved people's trust of the justice system. Having completed more than 1.9 million cases in over ten years, it is the most comprehensive program of post-conflict justice in the world.

I'm not suggesting that we gather random citizens, make them judges, and then govern ourselves. That's not what has happened in Rwanda, and that would be anarchy. I am saying that if we want to see more just systems, then we need more people in the community informed about our collective history, and we need more engaged citizens who are directly involved in the judicial and political processes. Any citizen in any state can offer education, register people to vote, make a phone call, sign a petition, or visit their congressional representatives. Some need to educate and organize their communities to this end; others need to raise funds, provide a meal or meeting location, or run for office.

What is your responsibility? The ways we choose to support the most vulnerable in our own communities can help us remember and bring unity.

A DEATH MARCH

I used to think of the wilderness as a perpetual death march—that the Israelites basically walked around in circles until a whole generation of people died off. That's only partially true.

God had given the Israelites direction and permission to enter the Promised Land. However, when Moses sent spies ahead, they returned with a bad report: the people were strong, the large towns were fortified, and there were giants in the land (Numbers 13:28-29). The hearts of the spies trembled with fear, and they concluded, "We can't attack those people; they are stronger than we are" (Numbers 13:31). Not only did they fear the giants, but their unwillingness to obey God also revealed the distorted view they had of themselves: "We seemed like grasshoppers in our own eyes, and we looked the same to them" (Numbers 13:33).

At this report, the Israelites cried out against God, Moses, and Aaron. Because they were unsure of the way ahead, they determined it was best to get a new leader and go back to the old system of slavery (Numbers 14:1-4).

Joshua and Caleb were the only spies who trusted God, and they offered a different perspective: The land is exceedingly good and abundant. The Lord will bless us with it if we don't rebel or fear the people in the land. They have no protection because God is on our side (Numbers 14:6-9). The Israelites responded by seeking to murder Caleb and Joshua, but the Lord stepped in (Numbers 14:10).

Instead of punishing the people with destruction, God forgave when Moses interceded. Yet there is always a consequence to sin. The Lord issued his judgment: aside from Joshua and Caleb, none of the male adults included in the first census in Numbers 1 would enter the Promised Land (see Numbers 26:62-65). Their dead bodies would fall in the wilderness; their children would become shepherds in the wilderness and suffer for the lost generation's unfaithfulness. The judgment would last forty years, one year for each day they spied out the land (Numbers 14:20-24, 28-35).

Those rebellious Israelites would not listen. They continued to sin against God, and God continued to purge them. The spies who brought the unfavorable report died of a plague (Numbers 14:37). When the Israelites complained about God's punishment at the revolt of Korah, Dathan, and Abiram, 14,700 more died of a plague (Numbers 16:41-50). Their leaders also fell: Miriam died at Kadesh (Numbers 20:1), and Aaron died for his lack of trust (Numbers 20:12, 22-29). Later the people had sexual relations with pagan worshipers, and another plague destroyed 24,000 lives (Numbers 25:1-9).

This is the way of the world—sin most certainly leads to death (Romans 6:23). We must remember.

For the Israelites, the wilderness was the place where a great community shift occurred. The Lord determined that the older generation of rebellious people needed to die off, and he needed to train the next generation how to reject the ways of their fathers and obey the voice of God. The deaths that occurred in the wilderness serve as warnings to remind us not to reject the ways of the Lord. Instead, we can remember his promises and his faithfulness, always wooing us to righteousness. We can allow him to cleanse our impurities and prepare us for what's ahead.

YOU SHALL LIVE AND NOT DIE

If we are going to come together and raise up the next generation, then we need to learn how to move about the wilderness. One of the earliest practical lessons I learned in the military was about the buddy system. The foundation of this system was understanding that we were a unit, a team, and a part of something bigger than ourselves, so we never went anywhere alone. If you were doing any extreme training or physical conditioning, you took a buddy because one of you might get injured and the other could call for help. If you went on leave, you took a buddy because somebody might get into a fight or get drunk or lost, and the buddy could fight alongside you, be a designated driver, or call a taxi if your cell phone ran out of juice. For centuries military personnel have been able to survive big and small battles simply because we don't go at it alone. We have a shared history, and we know that we need each other in the fight.

Who are your traveling companions in life? Who is there to lift you up when you are in dangerous situations or on the brink of death?

When Moses took the first census, at the beginning of the book of Numbers, he was preparing for war. But because that generation was not ready for real change, God essentially said, "Forget about them. I'm going to work among the people who will remember who I am and positively respond to what I do." In the wilderness God draws people who are lost and spiritually dead unto himself. He teaches and trains them; he reveals the historical narrative of creation, the fall, redemption, and restoration, and he invites them to enter into the story.

Once God restores his relationship with individuals, he makes it possible for them to become reconciled with other people. This reconciliation overcomes the fall and brings kingdom redemption. Then God sends his faithful out in teams to share the good news with others (see Mark 6:7; Luke 10:1). I'm so glad that God knew about the buddy system long before the Marine Corps did!

People are longing for shepherds to help them through the wilderness—to bring the rod and staff that comfort (see Psalm 23:4). Shepherds guide others as fellow sojourners. Shepherds are willing to look at the fallen bodies, say the names, share the stories, speak the truth in the wilderness. They aren't afraid to ask the relevant questions

> *People are longing for shepherds to help them through the wilderness.*

about how God wants to sovereignly enter into this period of history and what a person's role might be in that divine work.

We all need to answer some of the questions that seem to constantly confront the American people:

- Who is going to put an end to the violent system of racism?

- Who is going to fight for freedom and justice for all?

Answering these and related questions will cause us to see the giants in the land, and ourselves, differently. The choice is now before us, and we can choose life.

With their motto "Never Again, Never Forget," the Rwandan people have taught me that choosing life includes remembering and speaking the truth, even if that feels like I'm living as a foreigner, a pilgrim, or a sojourner in my own country. Cultivating this discipline of remembering and truth telling motivates us to prepare and build for the life of freedom that we want.

As I see God's kingdom more clearly, I am keenly aware of the dangers that are present in the Promised Land and in our modern world. When the Western way is not the way of God, I must reject it. When the Israelites did not see rightly after God brought them out of Egypt, he had to raise up a younger generation who would reject the ways of Pharaoh. Then God taught them how to live anew. If we desire to respond in obedience like the second generation of Israelites did, we need to remember and renew our minds. Surviving the wilderness requires us to have a different spirit, like the spirit the Lord put into Caleb (Numbers 14:24), so we can follow God wholeheartedly.

People are lining up for the census of those ready for a new way of life—a way that is just and equitable for all. Get ready if you want to be counted!

TRUTH IS: Remembering and telling the truth are essential if we want to come out of the wilderness together and live in communities where freedom and justice reign for all.

REFLECTION QUESTION: What is God calling you to remember or to put to death?

SCRIPTURE MEDITATION: "For the wages of sin is death, but the gift of God is eternal life in Christ Jesus our Lord" (Romans 6:23).

PERSONAL AFFIRMATION: I will live and not die in the wilderness!

CALL TO ACTION: Who are your buddies? Identify at least two people who get angry about the same injustice that you named in the last chapter. How can you encourage and support each other through the wilderness?

PRAYER: Lord, I thank you for graciously causing me to remember, even the hard things, when it is so easy to turn away or forget. I thank you that in the dark places you are teaching me how to live again. Help me to walk in this newness of life. In your Son, Jesus' name, amen.

TWEET: Remembering motivates us to train, prepare, and build for the life of freedom that we want. @asistasjourney #ASojournersTruth

CHAPTER TEN

HUMILITY

TRUTH IS, THERE IS HOPE
WORTH HOLDING ON TO

Am I sadly cast aside,
On misfortunes' rugged tide?
Will the world my pains deride
Forever?

GEORGE MOSES HORTON,
"THE SLAVE'S COMPLAINT"

W hat in the world were you thinking? When I tell you to ride the bus home, that's exactly what I expect you to do!"

These are the words I yelled to my brother after I peered out the window on a fall afternoon and saw him get out of the passenger seat of a car driven by a white girl. We'd just moved from Maryland to North Carolina. We didn't know anyone in town, and nobody knew him. But his tall figure, broad shoulders, and physique revealed his athleticism. I watched that tenth grader—a kid that news broadcasters would most likely call a man or maybe a thug—get out of the car where a tiny, cute blond girl stayed seated, and I prayed to God that she made it home safely.

I was mom now that my mother was gone, and it was time for yet another life lesson. So the lecture began: "What if something happened to that girl along way? What if she went missing, got beat up or raped? And you're the black stranger in town, the last person she was seen with? None of us have a reputation here. Who is going to vouch for you?"

Black parents don't like having these types of conversations with their kids, but there I was challenging my little brother—who wasn't so little anymore—to use some common sense. I don't know what was worse: fearfully knowing what would happen to him if the situation went south, or the humility of understanding my powerlessness to do anything about it.

God uses the hard realities of life to expose our deepest fears and internal struggles. These experiences make us more self-aware so we can cultivate the spiritual disciplines necessary to lead ourselves and others well.

LAMENT AND HOPE

Sad. Cast aside. Misfortune. Pain. These poetic words lament the hardships of being black and human in our fallen world. With a reality check and a wilderness lament, we acknowledge the separation between the world we currently live in and the world we want to experience—where all things are equal and all systems are just.

I want people like my brother to get the benefit of the doubt, for folks to presume he's innocent unless proven guilty. While I long for the redemption of broken systems, I don't put my hope in it. However, I do put my hope in God's ability to redeem people. I know it's hard to see in the wilderness, but redeemed people can create new systems. It seems idealistic, but we must anticipate and prepare for it.

Simon Walker speaks about the tension between what is and what can be in this way:

> [Leaders and idealists] have a desire for things to be different, to be better. Thus, the leader lives all the time with a discrepancy between the world that she wants (and wants

others) to inhabit and the world she (and others) actually do inhabit. Psychologists call this condition "cognitive dissonance"—there is a discord between the reality and the ideal. . . . Most people deal with the cognitive dissonance fairly effectively simply by choosing to look away from the ideal. They come to tolerate the reality by avoiding the evidence, by filtering the data they receive. They fabricate a world in which the discrepancy is less. The leader, however, is motivated by a desire to hold on to the ideal—indeed, it is the ideal that drives her. Accordingly, she commits herself to a journey that will inevitably lead her into a dissonance between the reality and the ideal, a tension that she refuses, until she gives up leading, to deny or suppress.

When living in a racialized society, it is so easy to look away, to avoid the mounting evidence, to filter the incriminating data that lands on our screens, and to fabricate narratives that make our world seem more just than it actually is. However, integrity of leadership—especially for the Christian—does not allow us to do so. Perhaps that is why leadership is often considered a lonely and isolating existence. For a true leader, settling for less than a better world, as we visualize it, simply will not do. So we press on through the tension and dissonance that we often feel.

Before we can pursue the ideal, we must first confront the discrepancies that the reality presents. Instead of minimizing those discrepancies, we analyze them: What do we do with all the broken spaces that don't measure up to our God-given, holy dreams? We also lament, grieve, and cry out to God. We plead on behalf of all who have lost hope, and we ask forgiveness for those who have caused us to accept the bitter lies.

Lamenting is a spiritual discipline, and doing so publicly can make us vulnerable. It's a practice in humility. Public confession also awakens us, and when done rightly and received well, it leaves no shame or guilt. What are the broken things in our society that you need to lament or publicly confess?

Confession leads to repentance, which puts us on the path toward a more hopeful future. Remaining hopeful sounds silly to the uninformed and unrepentant who cast aside the cries of the redeemed. I've found that being inspired by hope is also an exercise in humility. It's a choice to recognize that the facts, statistics, and history are not sovereign like God is. In the wilderness, I need to trust God over my intellect.

> *Confession leads to repentance, which puts us on the path toward a more hopeful future.*

Moses has taught me the need for persistence in choosing the ideal. This ordinary, teachable man humbly made himself available to serve God. When God looks to change a nation, he seeks people who will learn from him, be fully devoted to him, and not lose hope in the crucible of the wilderness. Intimacy with the Lord is what sustained Moses' work, and the Lord's presence gave him grace to deal with people who often did not understand him or his calling.

THE HEAVY BURDEN OF IDEALS

"You're fired. I'm sorry, but you are just not fit to lead in this capacity."

She looked at me across the table, and I could see a mix of sadness, disappointment, and resentment in her eyes. She put up a defense. I tried to explain that she'd received numerous opportunities to correct her behavior. I even invited her to continue serving with the ministry, but she would not listen to reason.

While I worked at the Naval Academy, one of my collateral duties was serving as the officer representative for the USNA Gospel Choir. That role included overseeing the choir's operations and mentoring its midshipmen leadership team. This midshipman was the president, and she didn't seem to understand that this role, like everything else at the school, was serving to prepare her for the real leadership, mentoring, organization, and service opportunities she would experience in the military fleet.

I knew the situation could have ended differently, but she took no ownership for her behavior, and that's why the final decision was made. As the officer representative I had worked to get the organization back in good standing with the school and raised money for them to travel again. The Gospel Choir was one of a very few predominantly black organizations on the campus. My responsibility was to make sure that it was professionally run in a manner on par with the rest of the music department and that we represented the school and black people well. The midshipmen didn't carry this same level of responsibility.

Even though this firing wasn't from a real job, no kids went hungry, and nobody lost benefits, her feelings were hurt and I felt bad. Leadership is a heavy burden.

Like Moses, you will find that as your responsibility to make a better world becomes clearer, the tension will rise in your own life. People will misunderstand your intentions or make assumptions about your motivations. They will scandalize your name. Some will criticize or seek to marginalize or silence you. Some will become jealous or covet your time and giftedness. Others may abandon you or even try to destroy you. If you've had these types of experiences, understand that the tension is often present because we live among and lead people who have seen the discrepancies but have chosen to look away. They don't want to take a hard look at themselves.

Firing the choir's president was one of several hard decisions I've had to make throughout my career, and making hard decisions about people and organizations that you love can take a toll on the soul. We begin to doubt, and sometimes without warning we can find ourselves in the midst of despair.

This is what happened to Moses, the humblest person on earth (Numbers 12:3). After the people complained about their misfortunes yet again in the wilderness, Moses was miserable. He cried out to the Lord: "What have I done to displease you that you put the burden of all these people on me? Did I conceive all these people? Did I give them birth? Why do you tell me to carry them in my arms, as a nurse carries an infant, to the land you promised? . . . If this is how you are going to treat me, please go ahead and kill me" (Numbers 11:11-12, 15).

Who would have thought that the humblest man in the world could fall so deep into despair? Have you ever found yourself in such a state of weariness? There are many days in my life when I find myself praying: "God, please don't let me become weary in doing good, for I know that at the proper time I will reap a harvest if I don't give up. Help me to press on and do good to all people, especially to those who belong to your family" (see Galatians 6:9-10). This prayer is particularly helpful when I'm going through a wilderness experience or dealing with difficult people. Prayer disciplines us to humble ourselves before God, and it also provides revelation for how to move forward.

> Prayer disciplines us to humble ourselves before God, and it also provides revelation for how to move forward.

I've rarely considered that being weary or miserable could also be a sign of pride. Yet Peter Kreeft makes this connection. He writes:

> Pride and despair are twin brothers. They do not exclude each other but encourage each other. There is a secret pride in despair—a tragic grandeur, an overweening claim unfulfilled —and there is a secret despair at being human in pride's demand to play God. Humility is the opponent of both. It keeps us from despair as well as from pride. The greatest virtue keeps us from the greatest vice.

Submitting to God through prayer, confessing our emotional condition, and growing in humility keep us from both despair and
pride when the journey to redemption seems slow.

AN INVITATION FROM JESUS

Whether you are parenting a teenager, correcting a college student,
running an organization, or mentoring a friend, the opportunity to
journey through the wilderness is a sacred invitation from God.
Even Jesus was led by the Holy Spirit to take this journey before
beginning his earthly ministry (Matthew 4:1-11). The wilderness
brings us to the humble path. It reminds us of the great charge to
take up our cross and follow Jesus (Mark 8:34).

I am thankful that I have people in my life like my spiritual
director who remind me of this invitation. I keep a quote from him
on the desk in my home office in a beautiful turquoise frame with
white vines, so I do not forget:

> As you grow in your giftedness; as more and more doors of
> opportunity open, the temptations of your enemy will increase.
> Your only hope, Natasha, to remain a good steward, is to em-
> brace your cross and take that downward path we so often
> talked about; the pathetic path brings death to you, but life to
> others (2 Cor. 4:12). In this way, you will become more and
> more like Jesus; the life that you'll live is the life of Christ Jesus.

There is nothing glamorous about the teachings of the wilderness. In solitude and isolation, we learn how to do the internal
work, how to surrender to God. And he teaches us how to lead
ourselves so we can effectively lead others on the sacred way.
Growing in humility gives us proper perspective. We soon realize
that reconciliation or redemption are not ours to bring about;
that's God's responsibility. If we respond in obedience to his invitation, we may experience the miraculous goodness and grace of

his transformation in our own lives. Then he can make us his ambassadors of reconciliation (2 Corinthians 5:20).

Our responsibility on the humble path is to tend to our assigned work, understanding that being a servant in God's kingdom is the first priority. The second priority is extending this invitation to other broken people on the path. What work has God assigned to you? Who are you inviting on the journey?

HUMBLY LEADING BROKEN PEOPLE

Maya Angelou's famous advice "When people show you who they are, believe them" resonates with many. At one point it seemed logical to me as well. When I looked at the history of the United States, my personal history, or even my leadership and ministry journey, I saw people who were sometimes hateful, selfish, greedy, or insensitive, and thus I concluded that's exactly who they were.

The problem with this life philosophy is that it's only partially true, and it was not helpful for those I observed or for me. My limited perspective may describe a person's characteristics, but it does not define their full identity. I've learned as an idealist that sometimes I just need to lower my expectations or change my view.

I'm so thankful for Bryan Stevenson's humble reminder that "each of us is more than the worst thing we've ever done. . . . If someone tells a lie, that person is not just a liar. If you take something that doesn't belong to you, you are not just a thief. Even if you kill someone, you're not just a killer." By God's grace, these same people can learn to tell the truth, to work so they do not lack, and to love instead of hate. We all need compassion and mercy. Our fallenness is a humble reminder of the power of God's grace, and that is our greatest hope.

While it is not our responsibility as leaders to shepherd everyone through all of their life and learning transitions, we do have a duty to speak truth, extend grace, exercise humility, love well, and allow time for people to grow—if we believe that God is still in the life transformation business. We are all broken, imperfect people called to serve broken, imperfect people.

The truth of Stevenson's words can help us get over ourselves. Each of us has our own mess to confess. When we see only the flaws people show us and incorrectly con- clude that's all there is to know about them, we have given up the blessed hope of understanding, learning, or seeking reconciliation. We have turned down Jesus' invitation to cultivate the intimate relationships that could change us and them. We have taken a pass on the pos-

We are all broken, imperfect people called to serve broken, imperfect people.

sibility that they will be any different, that we will be any dif- ferent—and so we lose confidence that we will ever learn to truly love each other. The work to overcome our misperceptions requires an extension of grace, and it requires humility from each of us.

HUMILITY THROUGH PRAYER

How often do you pray? We learn from Moses the same thing that we learn from Jesus: the secret to humility is praying and waiting for the Father's instruction. It's no surprise that Moses became a prayer warrior in the wilderness. Kreeft writes that prayer "is a kind of death, a rehearsal for death. In praying we die to ourselves, our wills, our ordinary consciousness and desires and concerns, even our ordinary world, and enter God's world, aligning our minds and wills with God's. We die to our time, we sacrifice our loaves and fishes to him. And he multiples them." Prayer is how Moses con- ditioned himself to respond to a holy God.

Pray, and don't give up on people. I've had to kill the thoughts that people don't want to commit to deep change, or that I can't trust or depend on anybody. These are lies from our common enemy,

Satan, to get me off the path or to keep me isolated. These lies can keep me from seeking or asking for help. They can keep me from trusting and building relationships and a better future with diverse people from all walks of life. What lies has Satan planted to keep you off the humble path?

Moses teaches us about cultivating a relationship with the Lord through prayer. Reggie McNeal writes that Moses "would come to find his greatest sense of belonging in his communion with the God of the burning bush. His constant sense of being an alien among those he lived with and served had carved out in his heart a huge place for God to inhabit." In prayer, God provided perspective and perseverance on the journey.

When Moses met God at the burning bush, he did not know what his leadership task would require of him. Being called to unforeseen challenges is not uncommon for God's servants, especially those who take on the weight of leadership. We see this in the long wilderness journeys of David, who was anointed king decades before taking the throne. We see it in the lives of Ezra and Nehemiah, who faced repeated opposition as leaders rebuilding their homeland. We see it in the life of John the Baptist, who cried out from the wilderness, "Prepare the way for the Lord" (Mark 1:3) before his head was chopped off and served on a platter. We see it in the life of Jesus, who spent forty days praying and fasting in the wilderness before embarking on his earthly ministry, which ended in his unjust conviction and capital punishment. We see it in the helpless waiting of every barren woman, in the isolated life of the widow and prophet Anna (Luke 2:36-38), and in the heartbreak of Mary as her son hung on the cross. The apostle Paul revealed his own life and leadership struggles to the church of Corinth (2 Corinthians 1:8-11).

Like Moses, Paul was able to lead his followers because he had been tried and tested through his wilderness experience. The hardship, suffering, and pressures of life, which often cause despair, did not break him. He prayed diligently and coveted the prayers of faithful people.

Humility teaches us that our earthly suffering is for one purpose only: that we might come to rely on God and not on ourselves. This is a critical lesson we learn in the wilderness.

TRUTH IS: Walking the humble path provides self-awareness and helps us cultivate the spiritual disciplines we need to lead others through the wilderness.

REFLECTION QUESTION: Which issues, people, and leaders are you led to pray for in this moment?

SCRIPTURE MEDITATION:

> [God] has shown you, O mortal, what is good.
>   And what does the LORD require of you?
> To act justly and to love mercy
>   and to walk humbly with your God. (Micah 6:8)

PERSONAL AFFIRMATION: Prayer is the way I will condition myself to respond to the Lord, who is holy.

CALL TO ACTION: Expose the lie. Stand on the truth. Make a two-column table. What lies do you most often believe about God and about people. List them on one side of the table. On the opposite side, list a biblical truth (with accompanying Scripture) that stands against that lie. Reference this list whenever you start to lose hope.

PRAYER: Lord, at times we are broken and heavy laden, and we need you. Even in the wilderness, remind us of your great redemption story. Like the cloud by day and fire by night, we need daily reminders of your presence and guidance in the desert. We are in desperate need, and we are dependent on you. Amen.

TWEET: Our earthly suffering is for one purpose only: that we might learn to rely on God and not on ourselves. @asistasjourney #ASojournersTruth

CHAPTER ELEVEN

TRUTH IS, WE MUST PREPARE TO FIGHT

To me, the language and symbols of religion
were nothing but weapons of war. I had
no other purpose for them. All the gods
are dead except the god of war.

ELDRIDGE CLEAVER, *SOUL ON ICE*

I love a good war speech, like the ones Mel Gibson performs in *Braveheart* and *We Were Soldiers*. In the movie *Glory*, Denzel Washington and the brave soldiers of the 54th Infantry Regiment allow us to eavesdrop on the camaraderie of a military unit that is going to war. Confession: I even tear up watching football scenes in one of my favorite movies, *Remember the Titans*. Coach Boone's (played by Denzel Washington) speech to the players at the Gettysburg cemetery and Coach Yoast's (played by Will Patton) speech during the regional championship game prepared players for the battle they would face together on the field.

War speeches let us know what's at stake, and they inspire us to reach for something greater. They remind us of who we are as a people and why we stand together and fight even if it costs us our very lives.

Faced with a long history of oppression and violence, we must acknowledge it for what it truly is: a spiritual war against the *imago Dei*. Even Dr. Martin Luther King Jr. used war language to describe his nonviolent tactics. He said, "This method has a way of disarming the opponent. It exposes his moral defenses. It weakens his morale, and at the same time it works on his conscience." King continued, "Even if he [the opponent] tries to kill you, you develop the inner conviction that there are some things so dear, some things so precious, some things so eternally true, that they are worth dying for. And I submit to you that if a man has not discovered something that he will die for, he isn't fit to live."

These are the facts: war is an ever-present reality, and we are all going to die anyway. Whether we seek it out or it comes to us, the presence of war requires that we consider the things we are willing to die for. As we ponder the cost of discipleship, Dietrich Bonhoeffer also beckons us to sacrifice our lives: "When Christ calls a man, he bids him come and die." I can still hear my mother saying, "Stand up for something, or fall for anything."

What are you willing to stand, fight, or die for?

FIGHTING A WAR OF OPPRESSION

The organized effort to defeat black people—who are perceived as dangerous or bad—meets the very definition of war, and the war strategy has evolved over the course of American history. From the first time my black ancestors stepped onto this land in 1619, our very existence, our right to belong, and our right to live as free people with innate dignity as God's image bearers has been a fight.

This war of oppression began with the institution of slavery, which the US Constitution affirmed. For generations the assault on black lives continued with legal lynchings. Bryan Stevenson, executive director of the Equal Justice Initiative, writes, "The true power of those lynchings far exceeded their number. They were acts of terror more than anything else, inspiring fear that any encounter with a white person, any interracial social misstep, any unintended slight, any ill-advised look or comment could trigger a gruesome and lethal response." The laws of Jim Crow instituted legal segregation between white and black Americans, including separate—but not equal—public schools, housing, and voting restrictions.

In the 1990s the government launched the war on drugs, which specifically targeted black and brown people. This war has helped to create a mass incarceration crisis. This crisis has been exposed by Michelle Alexander in her bestseller *The New Jim Crow*, as well as by film director Ava DuVernay in her award-winning documentary *13th*. Stevenson addresses this tragedy of mass incarceration:

> The extreme overrepresentation of people of color, the disproportionate sentencing of racial minorities, the targeted prosecution of drug crimes in poor communities, the criminalization of new immigrants and undocumented people, the collateral consequences of voter disenfranchisement, and the barriers to re-entry can only be fully understood through the lens of our racial history.

Stevenson concludes that the legal institutions of slavery, lynching, Jim Crow, and mass incarceration have drastically shaped American history and the way we view each other through the lens of "race." The idea of race has created a war of oppression with numerous casualties.

The good news is that every war eventually comes to an end. Normally wars end with the unconditional surrender of the losing side. Some end with a peace treaty; others, with the total destruction of the clearly defined enemy. If the racialized influence of legal institutions is a clearly defined enemy, then we must develop ways to defeat it. Public policy based on false perceptions about race is not something to yield to; it's something to fight against. Fighting may look different for each of us, but we must all agree to go after the enemy in our own way.

The church has been complicit in the problem. From the beginning of American history until now, the message has been reinforced that black lives do not matter—even in the church. This is why conversations about racial reconciliation cannot end with "Get a friend of a different race." That's a decent first relational step, but that's not justice. True racial reconciliation cannot exist without racial justice; therefore, we must educate ourselves about institutional systems in addition to individual actions.

The Christian faith speaks to the reconciliation of all division—between humans and God, within ourselves, in human relationships, and in our poor stewardship over the rest of God's creation. Reconciliation—bringing all of these things back into proper relationship—is a catalyst in God's redemption plan. We are in a spiritual battle, and history has proven that no long-term progress is made without a fight. I have decided that this war is one I am prepared to lace up my boots for, even if I perish.

> We are in a spiritual battle, and history has proven that no long-term progress is made without a fight.

TRAINING FOR WAR

"Sistrunk. Sistrunk, it's time to get up."

These were the words whispered in the wind as the bottom of my combat boots were being kicked. I squinted my eyes tightly and blinked a few times, trying to get my night vision.

It was only three o'clock in the morning, and the fall night's sky was hugging the tall maple trees. I sat several feet underground in a fox hole we had dug earlier in the day. We had already been in the field for a few days. I was surviving on adrenaline, lots of water, and packaged meals.

I sat in that hole all night long before the rain started to pour. I covered my weapon and myself with a poncho. Then I drifted in and out of sleep.

"Sistrunk, are you awake?" Second Lieutenant Hailey was rousing me because it was my turn to stand the late night watch.

"Yeah, yeah, I'm up!"

My foxhole buddy needed a verbal confirmation so he could get some rest. I leaned forward, positioned my sack against my back so I could sit upright, and spent the next three hours wiping my eyes and staring into utter darkness. I was miserable, but this is what our officer training consisted of at The Basic School in Quantico, Virginia.

With every map drawn, watch stood, patrol walked, and weapon fired, every push through physical and mental exhaustion, every woman or man trusted, and every hour of peak performance on little sleep, the Marine Corps taught me this: you will fight exactly how you train. And we were preparing to win a war.

My professional development manual informed me that "the purpose of training is to develop forces that can win in combat. Training in the key to combat effectiveness.... However, training should not stop with the commencement of war; training must continue during the war to adapt to the lessons of combat." In a very real sense, we learn how to fight well by getting in the fight, and taking stands in the wilderness provides great opportunities to do just that.

DEVELOPING A BATTLE PLAN

When the Amalekites attacked the Israelites, Moses executed his battle plan. He sent Joshua out to lead the fight as he went to the top of the hill and raised his staff—indicating God's fighting banner. When his arms got tired in the heat of battle, Moses sat down on a rock while Aaron and Hur lifted his hands, and this ultimately led to the Amalekites' defeat (Exodus 17:8-16).

With each wilderness battle we become more skilled. We learn to adjust our strategies and tactics along the way. Before we enter any battle, we must understand why we are fighting: What's the mission? How do we define mission accomplishment? Having this clarity helps us measure our progress and make the necessary adjustments so we know when we are winning. We must have a plan and prepare for war!

God gave the Israelites a mission to go to the Promised Land. They came out of Egypt armed for battle (Exodus 13:18), but they were not ready to fight. Initially the spies were sent to determine the best war strategy, not to discern whether or not they should go (Deuteronomy 1:22). But because they did not commit to God's mission, the majority of the spies were distracted by the opposition. They did not understand what the military specialist Sun Tzu knew: warfare is not simply a matter of force. It is not just about destroying an enemy physically; a true military leader must be concerned about unsettling their enemy psychologically. The ten Israelite spies did not trust God, and they had a poor view of themselves. That is why they were afraid and unwilling to undergo the basic training necessary to prepare them for war (Deuteronomy 1:20-33).

The Israelites defeated themselves psychologically, and that's what ultimately led to their failure. What are some lies you have believed about your own identity or ability to contribute to God's mission? In what ways have you seen our common enemy, Satan, his minions, and the structures-that-be as giants and yourself as a grasshopper (Numbers 13:33)?

If we want to fight in support of God's mission, then we must learn to win the battle in our minds. When our minds are recalibrated, we are removed from the life support of this world's ways and are plugged into a new reality—an awareness of our life as warriors in God's kingdom. Get your mind right! "Take captive every thought to make it obedient to Christ" (2 Corinthians 10:5). Be a warrior!

For us and for the Israelites, there is a clear reason to fight. We learn from the exodus narrative that God was using war experiences to set the Israelites apart as his holy people (Deuteronomy 7:6). Their preparation gives us insight as we face our own battles. Moses, their commander, provided the rules of engagement:

1. Do not be afraid of your enemy because God is with you (Deuteronomy 20:1).

2. The leaders must step up. Spiritual leaders (the priests) must first speak to the hearts of the people (Deuteronomy 20:2-4). Government leaders (the officers) must be prepared to answer the *What?* questions. In this case, the officials concluded that all of the people who were unprepared or too afraid to fight should go back because death was a real possibility and they could be a hindrance to the soldiers who were ready (20:5-8). Finally, the military or community leaders (the commanders, meaning those who had their boots on the ground with the people) must provide answers to the *How?* questions. These are the people who can put war plans into action (20:9).

3. The commanders' strategy was to go in peace at first. If the people of the land insisted on making war, however, the Israelites were instructed to take them over or kill them. If they didn't, these nations would lead the Israelites astray (Deuteronomy 20:9-18).

Note that this is the only instruction for holy war recorded in the entire Bible.

Israel's history serves as a warning to "keep us from setting our hearts on evil things as they did" (1 Corinthians 10:6). Their warfare humbles anyone who questions the seriousness with which a holy God views sin. When we are reminded of how far the human race has fallen, we must commit to standing on the side of the holy God, because the time to address blatant sin is always now. God called his chosen people to purge the sin from among them because if they didn't, they would become comfortable in it and the sin would overtake them.

Today, the New Testament informs us that our war is not against flesh and blood, "but against the rulers, against the authorities, against the powers of this dark world and against the spiritual forces of evil in the heavenly realms" (Ephesians 6:12). Therefore, we must prepare for war by "[putting] on the full armor of God, so that when the day of evil comes, [we] may be able to stand [our] ground" (Ephesians 6:13).

As I was reflecting on this Scripture in Rwanda, one of my spiritual mothers, Ms. Francine Pierson, reminded me that speaking the truth is an act of spiritual warfare. The belt of truth allows for self-care, for it wraps and protects our physical bodies. The breastplate of righteousness guards the heart so it cannot be penetrated. We must use our feet to take action and share the gospel of Jesus Christ, for it is written, "How beautiful are the feet of those who bring good news!" (Romans 10:15). The truth of the whole gospel brings peace. Ms. Francine reminded me that we must take up the shield of faith "trusting that God's Word will extinguish Satan's lies," and we put on the helmet of salvation because without it "your mind will not have the ability to understand spiritual kingdom principles." The sword of the Spirit is the Word of God, and when rightly divided, "it can cut through anything!"

Later on, one of the other mothers on the trip, Susan Seay, reminded me that in matters of injustice and warfare we must ask God: What is my place and position in this fight?

COMMITTING TO A STRATEGY

There is no authorization in the New Testament to kill anybody, let alone entire people groups. However, there is room for a practical strategy of "hitting people where it hurts." In a capitalistic society that expression has always meant attacking people's financial security. At the end of the day, institutions from slavery to the privatization of prisons and schools are about money. And by and large, that money is not lining the pockets of people of color. Furthermore, our laws—not just our individual efforts—determine who gets to develop forward-moving strategies and when.

Understanding the political systems at work is what made the Southern Christian Leadership Conference so effective during the civil rights movement. They marched with demands, and they boycotted because it allowed them to attack the system in multiple ways: bus companies lost money, white women lost the help of their nannies and housekeepers, and black people were prayerfully united and on mission. Many of our civil rights leaders sacrificed greatly because they had a strategic plan and farsighted goals. They were fully committed to the fight.

The problem we have today is that too many people choose convenience over progress. If a bank decides to charge an additional five dollars per month just because they can, people continue to bank there. If a school is not working for a child, people still keep the child in that failing system. If a favorite political party, sports team, or entertainer continually dishonors their values, people continue to vote for that party, watch that franchise, or make that person rich! If a job doesn't pay fairly, uses unjust work practices, or has a dishonoring work environment, they continue to work there because they don't have a vision for something better.

By submitting to broken systems, by not putting our money where our mouth is, and by staying silent when we are in desperate need of change, we prove that we have psychologically defeated ourselves and are not prepared to win. If we truly want victory and peace, then we have to inconvenience ourselves until we see real systemic change. And we have to make long-term commitments if we want

> *If we truly want victory and peace, then we have to inconvenience ourselves until we see real systemic change.*

to see these victories in our lifetime. What are you willing to give up? How will you take a stand and join in the fight?

Count the cost before you commit (Luke 14:28-32). Be wise. Learn some diplomacy. Don't just think about what you could lose in the fight; consider what might be gained!

Our war strategy is first spiritual and then manifests in the physical. We must first look to God, who goes before us in the fight:

Whenever the ark set out, Moses said,

"Rise up, LORD!
    May your enemies be scattered;
    may your foes flee before you." (Numbers 10:35)

When the Israelites destroyed the Amorite kings, Sihon of Heshbon and Og of Bashan, God was teaching the people how to fight (Numbers 21:21-35; Deuteronomy 2:24–3:11). He was granting them small victories to serve as a reminder that he was the one who fought their battles. There was no need for them to fear.

Moses did not let Joshua miss this point. He told him, You have seen with your own eyes how the Lord defeated these kings, and he will do the same to all who oppose you in the Promised Land. Do not fear. God will fight for you! (Deuteronomy 3:21-22). This psychological training gave Joshua the right perspective about God and the enemies he was up against, and that's how he prepared the Israelites for victory.

GET READY TO MOVE OUT

If we keep the right perspective in the wilderness, we realize that we really don't have anything to lose—not our reputations, our jobs, our homes, or important relationships. All of the false security of the past is dead to us. In God you don't have anything to lose, so train, prepare, and practice so you can fight well.

What is that buried hope that you have ceased dreaming about? What vision did the naysayers and haters put to death in you? The sojourn in the wilderness is when you go back to school to prepare for a new career, write your business plan, and build your team. In the wilderness you work your main job and your side hustle. In the wilderness you sacrifice income to pay off debt and save up so you can build something great for the future.

The wilderness is where you rally all the people who are ready and prepare them to fight. It's where you start teaching, tutoring, and mentoring children. Light up their eyes with the truth so they can know God and remember who they are. Arm yourself for battle, and lead the next generation into the land of promise.

TRUTH IS: We must prepare for war. We can win in this life if we have an accurate view of God, ourselves, and the enemy.

REFLECTION QUESTION: What are you willing to stand, fight, or die for?

SCRIPTURE MEDITATION: "But the Lord is faithful, and he will strengthen and protect you from the evil one" (2 Thessalonians 3:3).

PERSONAL AFFIRMATION: For God I live, and for God I will die.

CALL TO ACTION: What is the first step of resurrecting that hope, vision, or forgotten dream?

PRAYER: Lord, thank you for going before me in the heat of battle. You prepare me, give me the right words, and provide the strategy. Your Holy Spirit empowers me to fight. I'm so glad that you are greater than the evil one who is at work causing oppression, division, death, and destruction in the world. You make all things new, and you use ordinary people like me to do it. Arm me for the battles ahead so I can glorify you in the victories. In Jesus' name. Amen.

TWEET: Racial reconciliation talks must include a challenge to fight against racial injustice. @asistasjourney #ASojournersTruth

PART FOUR

REDEMPTION

*Surely goodness and love will follow me
all the days of my life,
and I will dwell in the house of the LORD forever.*

PSALM 23:6

Death comes before the resurrection.

When the miraculous resurrection happens, we must not be locked in our rooms (see John 20:19). Fear keeps us from seeing rightly, scrutinizing our history, reflecting on our wilderness experiences, looking into the face of Jesus, or walking where we have never gone before.

After surviving the wilderness we can tell the good news. We did not die! God is still speaking, Christ is risen, and that changes everything! The wilderness prepares us for redemption. From Adam to Abraham, Moses to David, John the Baptist to Jesus, the wilderness is where we learn to hear the messages of the redeemed.

God removed our blinders in the wilderness, and we received new sight. For God has chosen to hide the mysteries of his kingdom from those who consider themselves wise or prudent, and he has revealed his glory to those who humble themselves like little children (Matthew 11:25). We must learn to look toward the kingdom of God and pursue it in faith. This is what it means to live as a redeemed people. Will you look ahead to the promises of God's great kingdom and take the risk to enter?

CHAPTER TWELVE

TRUTH IS, WE CAN
FIND A WAY OUT OF
THE WILDERNESS

What was it that made me conscious of possibilities?
From where in the Southern darkness
had I caught a sense of freedom?

RICHARD WRIGHT, *BLACK BOY*

*I*t takes years for grief to settle into my bones. Although I was heartbroken for the families year after year, as bullet after bullet ripped into the flesh of Trayvon Martin, Jordan Davis, Michael Brown, and Tamir Rice, I carried on. At least I tried to carry on, knowing that my own brown-skinned brother was out there somewhere, and at any moment he could be lost to me forever. That is a reality worth grieving.

I slowly started to give myself permission to name it, write it, speak it, and get angry about it. When I spoke the truth out loud, it affirmed that many black people were suffering under the weight of this grief as well, so many of them in silence. In order for our breakthrough to come, we just needed to tell the truth.

I began to publicly tell the truth, mostly through my writing, when I realized that a whole new generation of black people had

been traumatized in this country, and I was among the many casualties of war. Many black leaders, entertainers, athletes, and other
people of influence started to do the same.

In 2016, I finally gave serious attention to Beyoncé. Although
she had sold millions of records, had won numerous awards, and
had a cult-like following, I did not jump on the "Beyhive" band-
wagon. However, the second single from her sixth studio album,
"Freedom," got my attention.

The visual album was as captivating as the music. We don't have
cable in my home, but we do have a gadget that allows us to
stream certain channels and shows. On this particular weekend
we also got the HBO channel for free. My family was scheduled
to attend an event, and I was already dressed to go. When they
came downstairs, however, I was halfway through watching
Beyoncé's album. I lay back on the couch and told them to go on
without me. I was mesmerized.

Over a heavy drum beat and bluesy guitar, she belted out the
lyrics:

> Freedom! Freedom! I can't move.
> Freedom, cut me loose!
> Singin,' freedom! Freedom! Where are you?
> Cause I need freedom too!

I couldn't take my eyes off of acclaimed ballerina Michaela De-
Prince as she danced so powerfully to these lyrics in her beautiful
white dress. I was familiar with her story. Born in Sierra Leone, she
lost both of her parents to the 1995 civil war. Because of her
vitiligo—a medical condition that causes discoloration of the
skin—she was abandoned by her family to an orphanage. There she
suffered abuse and starvation until she was adopted at age three by
a white couple from New Jersey. I watched her with every leap,
every plié, and every kick reject the lies—you are poor, ugly, the

devil's child—and false messages—you are unloved, unworthy, and unwanted—to let the world know that she was indeed well loved, alive, and free. You betta dance, honey! We are all watching.

"Freedom" is both a lament and a celebration song. It acknowledges what we all want: to live free or to die trying. This song acknowledges the darkness of the past and present, while demanding that each of us become better. Break the chains! Don't die! Press on. Don't quit! This is a message that black Americans desperately need, and Beyoncé isn't the only artist who has been socially conscious, taken a public stand against racial injustice, or offered inspirational songs that encourage forward movement.

FREEDOM SONGS

The advocate and artist Harry Belafonte once said, "When the movement is strong, the music is strong." Therefore, black singers in all genres have offered balms of healing and calls for freedom, such as Lecrae's track "Freedom":

> Freedom isn't free, but I still, I still believe
> In my freedom so my mind can see.
> Please let me be free.
> Please let me be free.

And Andra Day inspires us to rise again:

> I'll rise up
> I'll rise like the day
> I'll rise unafraid
> I'll rise up and I'll do it a thousand times again.

People, we can rise up for each other! In this music God is speaking, using his image bearers—some who claim to know Jesus intimately and others who do not—to offer hope to those who are holding on for dear life. James H. Cone wrote about the hope that liberation songs provide us: "Blacks found hope in the music itself—a collective self-transcendent meaning in the singing, dancing, loving, and laughing. They found hope in the stoic determination not to be defeated by the pain and suffering in their lives."

In the same tangible way, God used his words, his training, and the discipline provided in the wilderness to communicate a freedom message to the Israelites, who longed for a new life in the Promised Land. Could they live? To live freely, they needed to learn how to break away from their old ways of thinking and to reject the pagan ways of those who lived in the land they were going to occupy. They needed faith to believe, to press on, to persevere, and to rise up.

The Israelites' journey into the wilderness began with a liberation song:

> The Lord is my strength and my defense;
>   he has become my salvation.
> He is my God, and I will praise him,
>   my father's God, and I will exalt him.
> The Lord is a warrior;
>   the Lord is his name. . . .
>
> Who among the gods
>   is like you, Lord?
> Who is like you—
>   majestic in holiness,
> awesome in glory,
>   working wonders? (Exodus 15:2-3, 11)

With our songs and our dance, we are reminded that the entire journey in the wilderness forces us to stand in awe: Who is like the Lord? Nobody! This artistry beckons us to choose life by answering critical questions, such as, In the shadows of the history of the place we departed, and in light of where we are going, what shall we do? How will we enter into the new world?

When the enemy is doing everything possible to destroy your life, you must bring all of your tools to the fight. What tools and training do you need to break your wilderness chains? Now is the time to remind artists everywhere that the call for freedom requires freedom songs. Get your cadences and war songs ready. Grab your buddies. Write. Sing. Dance. Read. Act. Look up. Live free!

THE GIVER OF LIFE

The wilderness is where people start building for the place they are going, and for that they need the right perspective. As the older generation died off, God was raising up a new generation through the power of his word. Unlike manna, which normally provided physical nourishment only for one day, God's word would sustain them for a lifetime. This food, which they would come to know as "the law," was as important to them as the air they breathed because it taught them how to live as holy people before God. As Timothy Laniak wrote, "The most significant 'food' in the wilderness was the Law itself." There were 613 individual laws, but we will focus our attention on the Ten Commandments found in Exodus 20 and Deuteronomy 5.

Some New Testament readers consider the law a great burden. The apostles Paul and James lamented the difficulty of keeping it, while thanking God the Father for freedom through his Son (Romans 7–8; James 2:8-10). Jesus himself affirmed the law's significance by saying that he came not to abolish it but to fulfill it (Matthew 5:17-20).

The law was an expression of God's grace to a broken people, and it served as part of his redemptive plan so the Israelites could learn how to live holy lives that were acceptable and pleasing to him. Craig G. Bartholomew and Michael W. Goheen write, "Only as the Israelites obey God fully will they truly be a royal priesthood and a holy nation. Only as God's law shapes their whole lives will they fulfill their calling and be a blessing to the nations" (as God promised on oath to Abraham in Genesis 12:1-3).

With this purpose in mind, Klaus Bockmuehl identifies three functions of the Ten Commandments:

1. Civil use.

2. Accusing use.

3. Teaching use.

Bockmuehl explains,

> The Reformers said that whenever the Ten Commandments are preached or taught, some will be prevented from doing evil [civil use], some will be convicted and driven to Christ [accusing use], and some will be taught a practical lesson for daily living [teaching use]. They used three images to illustrate the three uses: a fence—to hem in the good, and keep out the bad; a mirror—to reveal the sinner in his nakedness and neediness; and a ruler—to mark out the standards by which the righteous shall live.

The Ten Commandments served to guide and set apart the Israelites while preserving the greatest good for all. On numerous occasions, God instructed the Israelites to love and teach this law to the sojourners and aliens living among them, and to treat them as native born because God does not show partiality (see Leviticus 19:33-34; Deuteronomy 10:17-19). God gave this instruction because he was building a new community of people who would live fully devoted to him. If everyone—young and old, female and male, Jew and Gentile, slave and free—obeyed the law to love God (as the first three commandments require) and to love their neighbor (as the remaining seven indicate), it would make for a better society. It would be virtuous if everyone acknowledged the Lord, and it would be great if no one murdered, committed adultery, stole, or lied to their neighbor. That's the type of society any moral human being would want to live in.

LEARNING HOW TO LIVE

It matters how we treat people who are different from us or outside of our normal social groups. God says, "Consider your neighbor in love." By giving the law, God showed that he cares about earthly things, including our earthly relationships. Whether the neighbor is of a different skin color, faith, socioeconomic class, or ethnic background, or whether they are an immigrant, foreigner, or undocumented worker, God says, "Consider your neighbor in love." Jesus said that the entire law of the Old Testament can be summarized in just two commandments: "'Love the Lord your God with all your heart and with all your soul and with all your mind.' This is the first and greatest commandment. And the second is like it: 'Love your neighbor as yourself.' All the Law and the Prophets hang on these two commandments" (Matthew 22:37-40).

The Ten Commandments teach us that the divine Word of God must have a physical impact here on earth. This is why Jesus prayed, "Your kingdom come, your will be done on earth as it is in heaven" (Matthew 6:10). There is a grave difference between how God thinks and runs things and how we determine what is best for our own lives. When we make self-centered decisions, we are not considering the other. People who think of themselves first are focused on how the old way of living affects them individually. Learning to live as God's people requires that we consider how a new way of living will affect us all collectively. For that we must draw near to God, and we must have a working knowledge of and proximity to "the other."

> Learning to live as God's people requires that we consider how a new way of living will affect us all collectively.

There was a time when my husband and I were one of only two black families that kept membership in a predominantly white church. During a personal interview the lead pastor asked me if I thought it was easier for a white person to join a predominantly black church or for a black person to join a predominantly white church. Without hesitation, I replied, "It's not at all easy! However, I do believe that people like us are more likely to join a predominantly white church, because as professionals we frequently work in environments where we are one of very few people of color in the room."

What I meant was that people of color—especially those who are educated, "white collar" professionals—are at least bicultural. We have learned to adapt, overcome, adjust, or assimilate as minorities because that is required in professional spaces if we want to become successful. People in the dominant group are not required to submit their will or make adjustments because they have the power to define normative behavior.

Far too often, white people either isolate or remove themselves from the opportunities God provides for them to become culturally competent in this way. People in the majority culture need to read, listen to, and learn from people of color. It is important for them to sit under the leadership of and have mentors who are people of color.

At the same time, people of color need to learn for themselves how to truly live free. We have been conditioned to see ourselves through the lens of the dominant people group. Now we must learn how to reject the desire for acceptance from the white majority, to reject the lies we have been told and the negative messages we have received about our beauty, our intellect, our families, our culture, our bodies, and even our own words.

WRITING TO LIVE

Acclaimed author Toni Morrison took ownership of her words. She rejected the perceived need for African Americans to respond to the "white gaze" or the white oppressor. She said, "What is the world like if he's not there? . . . There was this free space opened up by refusing to respond every minute to . . . somebody else's gaze."

I have pondered this same idea. I've wondered: Why did the words of white men have prominent placement in my university and seminary classrooms? Why is the white male's perspective—especially regarding history—the primary perspective that I received growing up in school? Why is the white male voice and experience dominating every Christian arena from journalism to publishing, from conferences to nonprofits, from the academy to pulpits, even in our multiethnic churches? The white male and his voice is not superior. Without this clear public service announcement, we will remain stuck in our old ways.

In his book *The Cross and the Lynching Tree*, James Cone wrestles with his Christian faith and white supremacy, and what that tension means for black people:

> In earlier reflections on the Christian faith and white supremacy, I had focused on the social evils of slavery and segregation. How could whites confess and live the Christian faith and also impose three-and-a-half centuries of slavery and segregation upon black people? Self-interest and power corrupted their understanding of the Christian gospel. How could powerless blacks endure and resist the brutality of white supremacy in nearly every aspect of their lives and still keep their sanity? I concluded that an immanent presence of a transcendent revelation, confirming for blacks that they were more than what whites said about them, gave them an inner spiritual strength to cope with anything that came their way. *I wrote because words were my weapons to resist, to affirm black humanity, and to defend it.*

I read this as I began work on this book. I read Cone because I wanted to, and also because I wanted my book to be saturated in the voices, words, and experiences of black people. And it was Cone, not any of the white men I read in seminary, who stood out among the faithful witnesses who helped me engage with this tension of race and the church.

Thank you, Sir. I've come to understand that for me writing is a spiritual discipline, a therapy of sorts. It is one of the ways that I communicate with God. Over the past few years I've committed to writing my way to freedom, casting a new vision, planning and strategizing a way of living and being as a disciple of Christ in a fallen world—a disciple who is fully black, fully woman, fully known, fully loved, and fully empowered by the Holy Spirit. Every day, I choose to live free!

I don't just write for myself. I use my pen, or mostly the keys of my laptop, as a weapon of war—to resist, to affirm our common humanity, and to defend it. I write for communities who are down-trodden and in desperate need of the liberation that only God can provide. I write for people whose conscience tells them that something is not right but in humility can confess that they don't know what to do about all the brokenness. I write for people who long to embrace the love of Jesus but are perplexed by the hypocrisy of his church. I write for the people who are committed to figuring it out together.

> *What if we all learned a new way, and what if we were not afraid?*

What if we all learned a new way, and what if we were not afraid? What if we truly lived redeemed?

BRINGING GOOD THINGS TO LIFE

I appreciate that James W. Sire began a chapter of his book *Discipleship of the Mind* with the subtitle "Bringing Good Things to

Life." There he offers guidance for dealing with technology, but I believe his six principles are also generally applicable for living a redeemed life:

1. Let God's Word guide the ways we develop our character and deal with each other.

2. Understand that we need a change of heart, which includes humbling ourselves before God and others, before we can develop the right strategy. Humility comes before the action.

3. We need to have proper context for the issues we are trying to address. "Every Christian should know a little bit about almost everything; some Christians should also know a lot about many things; others should strive to know all there is to know about a very few things."

4. We need to have conversations with Christians who share our similar concerns. Listen well to find out what they're thinking.

5. Do not act based on incomplete information. Keep an open mind. Become a humble searcher before you attempt to become a teacher or activist.

6. Once you become an informed activist, respect others as made in the image of God regardless of whether you agree with them.

These instructions provide good guidelines for living in a pluralistic society. To carry them out we need to discover the significance, truth, and wisdom of God's Word. God's Word—both the written and the incarnate—will light a new path for us to walk toward redemption (see Psalm 16:11; 119:105). The Word gives life!

We can allow God to give us a new vision for the future. We need an attitude adjustment regarding all the nations or people groups that the Father has invited into his kingdom. Humility, with a willingness to listen, learn, and draw near to God, can drastically shape the way we view others. Listening to people without being defensive is an important life skill, and understanding broader contexts is key if we truly want to break away from the old path. We can incline our ears to hear from different voices and consider different perspectives, even when we don't all agree.

Become a humble searcher, a student first. This is the true nature of discipleship: first look to Jesus, then follow, and eventually open your mouth to teach and invite others along to proclaim the good news. Seek first the kingdom of God and his righteousness (Matthew 6:33). Jesus has modeled the way of love. Let him guide us to freedom.

TRUTH IS: God's inspired Word and his inspired people guide us out of the wilderness and release us to walk into a new way of life.

REFLECTION QUESTION: What people of color do I need to pay attention to at this point in my faith and leadership journey?

SCRIPTURE MEDITATION: Because the Israelites did not obey God's Word, they could not remain in the land of promise but eventually went into exile. God gave the prophet Ezekiel a vision of a valley of dry bones, which represented exiled Israel. God promised:

> My people, I am going to open your graves and bring you up from them; I will bring you back to the land of Israel. Then you, my people, will know that I am the Lord, when I open your graves and bring you up from them. I will put my Spirit in you and you will live, and I will settle you in your own land. Then you will know that I the Lord have spoken, and I have done it, declares the Lord. (Ezekiel 37:12-14)

PERSONAL AFFIRMATION: I will obey the Word of the Lord, and live!

CALL TO ACTION: What three authors, artists, preachers, or leaders will I seek to learn from this year? Consider people of color who are serving: one locally, one nationally, and one internationally.

PRAYER: God, you often place before us two choices—death or life. Sometimes we choose death because it appears that we are winning, but we don't realize that we are like zombies. We are dead when blinded by our own sin and self-interests. We are dead when consumed by the schemes of the evil one. We are dead when we harbor hatred in our hearts against others. Help us to live free or to die to ourselves while trying. Give us enough confidence in you to take the risk to love, to listen, and to learn. In Jesus' name, Amen.

TWEET: We can allow God to give us a new vision for the future. @asistasjourney #ASojournersTruth

CHAPTER THIRTEEN

TRUTH IS, YOU NEED THE RIGHT PEOPLE AND PERSPECTIVE

Whoever hopes for the great things
in this world, takes pains to attain them;
how can my hope of everlasting life be well grounded,
if I do not strive and labor for that
eternal inheritance?

RICHARD ALLEN, "A PRAYER FOR HOPE"

I remember seeing her—I'll call her Miss Kingdom-leader —standing at the podium speaking in front of a group of her peers for the first time. She was only eleven years old, the youngest student in our "Walk in Purpose" Leadership Summer Program for Girls. Through this program, leaders within my nonprofit, Leadership LINKS, Inc., intentionally encourage and equip the next generation for innovation, entrepreneurship, and executive leadership.

As an African American middle school student, Miss Kingdom-leader came to us with a lot of uncertainties about herself. She was smart and beautiful, yet she had doubts about what she could and could not do. As mentors in the program, we started speaking life and truth in the face of her uncertainty and the false messages from the world that she had picked up along the way. We oriented this tribe of girls to face their fears, grow in confidence, rise to any occasion, and take the risk to see themselves as leaders. Because we are citizens of a new kingdom, we also challenged them to do this together and for others.

Throughout the week of the program, Miss Kingdom-leader worked with her team to create a business plan to offer a product or service that addressed a community need. The team knew that they had to present their plan to a panel of adult judges for evaluation on Friday. Normally the teams that perform best are the ones that share the work and presentation responsibilities. From her pre-program evaluation, we knew that she dreaded public speaking, so she and all the other girls were given opportunities to practice throughout the week.

Miss Kingdom-leader ended up being on the winning team! During our closing ceremony, that team was given a bigger stage to present their business plan to parents, educators, and community leaders. Afterward, I asked Miss Kingdom-leader, "When did you get over your fear of public speaking?" To which she sweetly replied, "Tuesday."

On a very practical level, that is the power of mentoring and sponsorship. We all need someone to create opportunities for training and growth, and to introduce ways for us to live into the endless possibilities available in the new kingdom. Knowing, believing, and seeing what's possible—actually having someone mentor and model the way—is half the battle to living anew. From generation to generation, the kingdom of God advances through faithful people who raise up the faithful, disciples who make disciples, and mentors who multiply.

BUILDING FOR A NEW KINGDOM

Offering mentorship and sponsorship are two ways we can exercise our redemptive influence to cultivate learning communities that facilitate the shared values of kingdom citizenship. Moses teaches us that building with a God-sized mission and influence takes a team approach. During the exodus and wilderness sojourn, Aaron and Miriam shared in Moses' leadership. Aaron was the voice box, and Miriam led as both prophetess and praise warrior (Exodus 4:14-16; 15:20; Micah 6:4). When Moses grew tired, God sent his father-in-law, Jethro, to show him how to delegate tasks to community judges (Exodus 18:5-22).

To an extent, I maintain hope to persevere and labor for the new kingdom because I am greatly encouraged by older saints—those in the Bible, like Moses, and the elders and mentors in my life, like Mrs. Patricia Raybon. From them I glean wisdom and perspective.

I smile whenever I think about one conversation I had with Mrs. Raybon. We two African American women—she from one generation and I from another—were talking about the ministry of writing and platform building. We both see the former as ministry and work but don't particular enjoy the latter. Yet I remember her looking through my computer screen on a video conference, encouraging me to move forward, and reminding me that God is my sponsor.

You must remember—when you are filled with uncertainty and doubt, when you are unsure about the way ahead in the new kingdom because you have never seen it before—that God is your sponsor! He is the one who opens doors for you that no one can shut. He is the one who takes your name and elevates it. He introduces you to the right people. He sets all things right. He has put the right spirit within you so you can withstand the resistance and spiritual darkness of this world.

In the next generation of Israelites after Moses, Caleb was able to see rightly, follow God wholeheartedly, and encourage the Israelites to enter the Promised Land the first time because he had the right spirit (Numbers 14:24). The right builders in God's kingdom are always those who are filled with the Spirit: "If anyone does not have the Spirit of Christ, they do not belong to Christ" (Romans 8:9). They are also those who are willing to sacrifice and bear the burden of the people so their faith can be realized. God's kingdom is revealed through them. They are the ones who serve as mentors and sponsors for the next generation.

A critical part of establishing the new kingdom was the mentoring relationship between Moses and Joshua. Joshua served as Moses' assistant for forty years, and that mentorship was Joshua's training ground and God's succession plan. Moses also served as a sponsor: because he took or invited Joshua nearly everywhere he went, Joshua was able to glean from Moses' authority.

We need people in every generation who will educate, guide, and navigate for others. Those are some of the responsibilities of mentors. A mentor cultivates a relationship; they learn you and your story well and offer perspective for how that story fits within the context of God's great redemption story. And they are willing to journey with you on the road.

Sponsors, on the other hand, are the people who open doors and create opportunities to get you where God wants you to contribute. They are further along on their journey, so they get invitations and access to events, programs, networks, and opportunities when people on your level are not invited. Yet when sponsors go into those select rooms and enter into new networking relationships, they take your name and your story with them. They are setting you up for good! When building for a new kingdom, we need both mentors and sponsors.

WHY ARE MENTORING
AND SPONSORSHIP IMPORTANT?

The old system is rigged. Our country was built by white men on stolen land, with free or cheap labor. The many contributions of people of color are often overlooked, their history erased, and their stories infrequently told. Rarely do they have the opportunities to lead or benefit from their own creativity and innovation. For centuries, people of color have been faithfully praying, educating, advocating, and working against this old system, but in every area of life the structures of inequality remain. Even when people of color earn titles, they are often not paid fairly. When they are invited to serve on boards, their voices are often silenced or they may not have the right to vote.

We must dig deeper to determine where the real power and biases lie. Then we must confess that access and opportunities for leadership and ownership are often delayed or denied for people of color. This is a kingdom issue!

I was not shocked to read attorney and diversity life coach Helen Kim Ho's article "8 Ways People of Color Are Tokenized in Nonprofits." She writes that nonprofit organizations typically work in this way:

1. They recruit people of color (POC) to formal leadership positions, but white staff keep all the power.

2. Their paid staff in charge of messaging are white, while volunteer storytellers are people of color.

3. They hire people of color only for "POC stuff."

4. They create and maintain an organizational culture that promotes white dominance.

5. They convene special "diversity councils" but don't build POC leadership on their main board.

6. They use people of color as a mouthpiece or shield against other people of color.

7. They give more money to white-led nonprofits, even when the nonprofit is focused on people of color.

8. They intuitively know the nonprofit space would benefit from more POC leaders, but they don't really know why.

We see these tokenisms at work in every professional arena, and even in the Western church.

The truth is, we are all impacted by biases. So building for a new world means naming and then intentionally addressing implicit biases. Implicit bias is "the bias in judgment and/or behavior that results from subtle cognitive processes (e.g., implicit attitudes and implicit stereotypes) that often operate at a level below conscious awareness and without intentional control." The subconscious processes are affected by our developmental history, life experience, culture, and the ways we view ourselves. Sociologists and social psychologists tell us that we all have a positive attitude toward the things that are familiar to us and people who are most like us. Therefore we need exposure to more diverse people, even in our mentoring and sponsorship relationships, so we can explore some of our commonalities in addition to understanding our differences.

Building for a new world means naming and then intentionally addressing implicit biases.

Redemption requires repentance for our part in broken systems, and then we must rebuild. We need a progressive reformation of our entire community and culture, including the church. The word *progressive* is not for liberal or political use here. C. S. Lewis wrote, "We all want progress. But progress means getting nearer to the place where you want to be. . . . If you are on the wrong road, progress means doing an about-turn and walking back to the right road; and in that case, the man who turns back soonest is the most progressive." Repentance—turning from the wrong to the right road—changes the course of human history.

Jesus has ushered in a new kingdom. In his kingdom, many of those positioned last will receive first place, and the first will be last (Matthew 19:30; 20:16). In his kingdom, both daughters and sons are invited as prophets, while the old and young are both filled with dreams and visions that need development (Acts 2:17). In his kingdom, those from every tribe, language, and people group or nation will exist to serve him together.

God is constantly birthing people into this world who reject the status quo, who look beyond the history, statistics, and facts to see what he has purposed in the spiritual realm. Throughout generations, by the power of the Spirit, this now and not-yet kingdom expands in the physical realm through the witness and work of ordinary people who pledge their allegiance to the real King. Invite this redemptive power to infuse every part of your life!

HOW MENTORING AND SPONSORSHIP EQUIP US

I couldn't wait until Margot Shutterly's *New York Times* bestseller *Hidden Figures* came to the big screen because it was an opportunity to learn about the significant contributions of the African American women at NASA. I had not read the book, but I saw the movie trailers and started familiarizing myself with this forgotten part of American history. I went to see the movie alone during opening weekend, then returned to the theater with my then nine-year-old daughter. Several weeks later, when her grandparents visited us, our entire family journeyed across town to enjoy the movie together in recliner chairs with popcorn and sodas because we wanted the full experience. There we were—three generations of black people in America—mesmerized that one of our long-forgotten stories was now being told with such beauty, boldness, and grace.

These pioneers of NASA faced what is referred to as "intersectionality": they fought against injustices for being both black and female, and they succeeded through peer mentoring and by sticking together. Because mathematician Katherine Johnson was the only heroine from the story who was still alive at the time of the movie's release, much of the movie's promotion centered on her life and legacy. However, I was most impressed with Dorothy Vaughn's character.

Dorothy Vaughn became the first black supervisor at the National Advisory Committee for Aeronautics (NACA, which was replaced by NASA in 1958). She had a tenacity for self-learning, mentorship, and lifting others up as she climbed. Whatever Dorothy learned, she taught. Whatever she had, she shared. This is the way of being and building when you lead and serve from a place of abundance, not of scarcity. When given the opportunity to receive a promotion, Dorothy refused to accept it unless the other black women who served on her team could go with her. Dorothy served her community as both sponsor and mentor, and we can all learn a lot from her. In the new kingdom, we need Dorothy's kind of knowledge, awareness, perseverance, selflessness, sacrifice, and generosity in every arena.

I've been mentored by dead people through books. Learning stories like these, even through the mediums of movies and books, enlightens us and raises our consciousness about who can do what well. Learning how to build for a new world requires that we make connections between what is possible (by the grace of God this can be done), what is historical (it has already been done by these people), and what is factual (you have the ability to do it) so we can remove the barriers and provide access for any able person to get the job done. Only then will we start to see, expect, and chart a new way ahead.

WHAT TO BUILD?

"What are you thankful for?" We were wrapping up one of our mentoring sessions, and this was the final question asked during our time of sharing. Each of the girls in our Leadership LINKS Mentoring Program was given the opportunity to respond.

One of the LINKS leaders said, "I'm thankful for this program." When a peer asked her, "What do you like so much about being here?" she replied, "I feel welcomed and accepted." Going down the line, one mentee responded, "I am thankful that this program has given me the opportunity to prove myself." Without fail, we have seen that mentorship and sponsorship have the power to change a person's self-perception and the way others view them.

In addition to changing perceptions, mentorship and sponsorship give us the confidence to take risks and try new things. Through my nonprofit, we are intentionally cultivating a multigenerational and intercultural community where women and men can lead together. There young people can see what a redemptive model of male-female relationships and leadership looks like—a environment without ego and competition, where the focus is not on who has the most power, who has the final say, or who is in charge.

In the new kingdom, we learn to submit to God and to each other out of our reverence for Christ (Ephesians 5:21). Together we mentor and multiply for God's kingdom. I came to tears during the closing ceremony of our 2017 leadership summer program because I was serving and standing shoulder-to-shoulder with friends who had mentored me and people I had mentored for years, and now we were mentoring the next generation together.

You may not start a nonprofit, but you can mentor by serving, giving, leading, teaching, or sharing your passion with others. You have some level of skill or influence that gives you the power to sponsor someone. You can cultivate a loving environment for people of all ages to connect and grow together.

To effectively build for the new kingdom, you must also educate yourself. Broaden your scope of reading and listening. If you are part of the majority culture, read books written by people of color and watch documentaries and movies written and produced by people of color. Then share what you have learned. Rally your peers and build a community of kingdom-minded people so that you can all purposefully grow in wisdom, knowledge, love, and service together.

At the end of the day, we all need to invest in and cultivate a sacred community that reflects the goodness and glory of God. Consider:

- Who can I mentor or sponsor?
- What kind of community do I want to be a part of, and how can I help shape it?
- What skills, gifts, and talents can I share with others?

Know that you have something to contribute. When God created you, it was with purpose and value (see Genesis 1:27; Psalm 139:14-16; Jeremiah 1:5). There are no weak or dispensable parts in the body of Jesus Christ, for "God has placed the parts in the body, every one of them, just as he wanted them to be" (1 Corinthians 12:18; see also 1 Corinthians 12:4-6). How will you, as our Leadership LINKS creed states, "actively take part in the great work God is doing in the world"?

THE RIGHT FOUNDATION

When people like Miss Kingdom-leader are shaped through mentoring and sponsorship, their foundation gets shaken. Old stuff is uprooted. We need this pulling and unsettling in our personal lives and in our broken systems.

The six founders of Leadership LINKS, Inc. are all African American. From the moment of our founding, that dynamic was a source of tension for me. I am aware that having a high-quality education organization that is predominantly led by African Americans makes some folks nervous, and I know others incorrectly assume that the programming and services we offer are just for African American students. In the old system, by contrast, it is "normal" when organizations are led by all-white leadership, and far too few people question that norm.

Given the foundation of our country and its history, we need to celebrate when people of color take on the responsibilities of ownership and leadership. We all need to create sacred and safe learning spaces where people of color can assert their God-given identity with dignity and respect. This gives those in the dominant people group the opportunity to learn from, be mentored by, financially support, and submit to the leadership of people of color. This is not a threat to the God-given identity of people in the dominate group. On the contrary, they will greatly benefit from being mentored by people of color. This relationship can give majority-group mentees great opportunity for spiritual growth and maturity—for God to remove blind spots, encourage humility, and advance the kingdom of God—without them assuming the dominant position over minority people.

In his new kingdom, God is calling us to reject the ways of the world by building more diverse learning environments. Henri Nouwen writes about the significance of this redemptive work:

> The task of future Christian leaders is not to make a little contribution to the solution of the pains and tribulations of their time, but to identify and announce the ways in which Jesus is leading God's people out of slavery, through the desert to a new land of freedom. Christian leaders have the arduous task of responding to personal struggles, family conflicts, national calamities, and international tensions with an

articulate faith in God's real presence. They have to say no to every form of fatalism, defeatism, accidentalism, or incidentalism that makes people believe that statistics are telling us the truth. They have to say no to every form of despair in which human life is seen as a pure matter of good or bad luck ... and proclaim in unambiguous terms that the incarnation of God's Word, through whom all things came into being, has made even the smallest event of human history into kairos, that is, an opportunity to be led deeper into the heart of Christ.

Building equitable spaces is a necessary, sacred, and monumental task.

Connecting with "the right people, in the right place, at the right time" helps us build for a new kingdom. Being awakened to injustices, paying attention to the voices that are missing or the stories that are untold, and considering the "other" who we think we do not need (see 1 Corinthians 12:14-27; James 2:1-9) equips us to mentor and sponsor in God's kingdom.

> God is calling us to reject the ways of the world by building more diverse learning environments.

This is the way we build: lay a new foundation, create and tell new stories, dismantle old systems, and build equitable ones. Gathering a community that is committed to building in God's kingdom in a way that benefits all people takes lots of work, and with great work comes great reward. Let's build anew!

TRUTH IS: We need mentors and sponsors to build in the new kingdom.

REFLECTION QUESTION: What are you building for the new world? Who are your community partners?

SCRIPTURE MEDITATION: "By the grace God has given me, I laid a foundation as a wise builder, and someone else is building on it. But each one should build with care" (1 Corinthians 3:10).

PERSONAL AFFIRMATION: I will mentor and multiply for the glory of God's kingdom.

CALL TO ACTION: Right now, you have the choice to mentor or sponsor someone. Who will it be?

PRAYER: Lord, according to your divine power, you have given us everything we need for a life of godliness (2 Peter 1:3). You have prepared me to build with your kingdom focus and vision in mind. Thank you that I do not have to go at this work alone. You are with me, and you have already connected me to the right people. Help us to live and build together as your redeemed. In Jesus' name, Amen.

TWEET: Building for a new world means naming and then intentionally addressing implicit biases. @asistasjourney #ASojournersTruth

CHAPTER FOURTEEN

TRUTH IS, LOVE WILL
LEAD US HOME

Baptize me . . . now that reconciliation is
possible. If we're gonna heal, let it be glorious.

WARSAN SHIRE, "FORGIVENESS"

Natasha, what do you do for fun?" That's the question one of the deacons of my church asked while we were out on a double date. For much of that year, people only saw me working, traveling, and working some more. I get quite a bit of pleasure out of my work, the people I work with, and those I influence. However, there are times when rest is needed, and self-care is necessary for sustainment.

I wear a lot of hats—business owner, nonprofit leader, author and advocate, wife, mom, friend—so the daily discipline of intentionally showing up or being present to life's responsibilities and relationships can feel overwhelming. I haven't always acknowledged my own fatigue or wounds, or recognized my need for healing. I am growing in understanding the importance of self-care by keeping basic spiritual disciplines such as resting, honoring the sabbath, and occasionally going on a spiritual retreat. Keeping regular habits like working out, enjoying the discipline of celebration through laughter, or hanging with friends has also encouraged the healing process.

In response to my friend's question that day, I said, "Girl, I just enrolled in a dance class!" I continued, "I've always enjoyed dancing. I took formal lessons as a kid. By the time I was in high school, I was learning the latest dance crazes and practicing them in the night club. College didn't allow for such pleasantries, and then adulting nearly took the dance away from me." Thank God that my daughter and the Michael Jackson Wii game have allowed me to participate in the simple joy of dancing. When I learned about an adult class where I could practice tap, contemporary, and liturgical dance, I jumped at the opportunity.

For those of us who are so focused on our work and generous with our time, we must remind ourselves that God gives everything for our enjoyment (1 Timothy 6:17). Therefore, without shame, guilt, or a false sense of selfishness or indulgence, we must find the healing, joyous, and purely delightful things that reveal the glory of God's redemption to ourselves and to others. If not, we will lose our way, burn out, or even become bitter.

THE LORD WHO HEALS

As Moses neared the end of his life, he became bitter. In the book of Deuteronomy Moses states on three separate occasions that God would not allow him to enter the Promised Land because of the people (Deuteronomy 1:37; 3:26; 4:21). You can almost hear the pain and resentment in his voice: "I will die in this land; I will not cross the Jordan; but you are about to cross over and take possession of that good land" (Deuteronomy 4:22). The truth is, Moses did not enter the Promised Land because he did not honor God (Deuteronomy 32:48-52), yet he was blaming the people for his own actions.

After Moses' death the Israelites crossed the Jordan River, and for them it was a baptism of sorts. They entered the water fearful and anxious about what awaited them on the other side, and they exited to walk into a new life. They renewed their covenant relationship with the Lord and followed the leadership of Joshua. A generation of people went on to serve the Lord beyond Joshua's death at age 110 and throughout the lifespan of the elders who outlived him (Joshua 24:29-31). Moses missed out on this glorious celebration.

It's not difficult to understand how leading a group of rebellious people can make anyone bitter. Yet it was God who reminded his people that even bitter water can be made sweet. He assured them, "I am the LORD, who heals you" (Exodus 15:22-26). Part of our healing includes embracing the opportunities and choices God provides for us to grow in love. Therefore, let's consider the healing actions that can guard our hearts against bitterness.

Throughout their exodus journey, God tested Moses and the Israelites. The Israelites could not worship God on their own terms, and they could not worship God while also defending their right to worship idols. God alone would set the standard for their holy living. By following God, the people made a choice for redemption. Redemption includes our healing; yet there is always a cost, and the cost is that of love.

Do we love God enough to follow and obey him? Obedience is the true mark of our love (John 14:15, 23; 15:10; 1 John 2:3; 5:3). Only when we truly learn to love God can we learn to love ourselves and each other rightly (1 John 4:7-12; 5:2).

LOVE THYSELF

As a black woman, I've had to learn ways to love and care for myself differently in God's kingdom. The culture of black matriarchs is to care for and prioritize everyone but yourself. As I love, lead, and mentor others, I am learning how to resist that temptation because it leads to psychological stress, compassion fatigue, poor physical and spiritual health, and even trauma. Part of my spiritual formation is being honest with myself about the stress, learning to set healthy boundaries, and giving myself time to heal. Of this need for self-care, activist Bree Newsome writes:

> Images and conversations depicting me as black female superhero are amazing and empowering, but they also remind me that black women are often called upon to demonstrate superhuman strength, usually to the detriment of our health and well-being. We're living in a society that was built upon the enslavement and dehumanization of black people, a society that targets black women in specific and heinous ways. Being intentional about caring for ourselves and each other and carving out moments and spaces for joy is itself a radical form of resilience and resistance.

My self-care has included celebrating, supporting, amplifying, and building communities with women of color. For you it might look totally different. Self-care gives us all a joyful resistance and resilience so we can live healthy and not 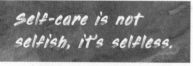 die prematurely. I want to continue on this redemptive journey for a long time, and that's why caring for my physical body, emotional health, relationships, and soul is necessary. Self-care is not selfish, it's selfless.

Get out of the house and out of your office. Take a walk or a day of rest at a park. Consider reading a great book for pleasure, lying out in the sun, or going for a hike, if that's your thing. Lose yourself in a song or dance. (Yes, I'm the girl that you honk at for not moving when the traffic light turns green because my eyes are closed and I'm singing my favorite song at the top of my lungs.) Don't wait for an invitation to heal. Take yourself out on a spontaneous date or initiate a night on the town with friends. Laugh until your belly aches; eat ice cream sometimes; savor the last cookie. Remember that you are still alive. Loving and caring for one's self creates a shift in the body, soul, and mind and sets an expectation of how others can love you. That's relational.

To find the redemption and healing that is needed for our systems, we must also change our minds concerning the old, broken way. I've learned how to play the professional games that were necessary for survival. The problem is, I don't want to just survive in this life; I want to thrive, flourish, and live free! Giving myself space for healing and regeneration has been a gradual process toward this end. It has included stepping away from traditional jobs and making moves to trust God completely. It has meant asking for help, going to counseling, and seeking spiritual formation. It has included removing chemicals from my hair and allowing it—and me—to move about the world just as natural, free, and strong as the Lord made us.

Healing has meant gaining confidence in my own voice and trusting the gifts, passions, and convictions that God has placed within. It has included stewarding my work and platform well. Being an African American woman with the gift of leadership in a church system that is dominated by white, male voices presents its own unique challenges. Additionally, my commitment to pursuing reconciliation, justice, and equity for women and the impoverished, my convictions regarding orthodox teaching, and my resisting false narratives about evangelicalism mean that I am somewhat of a pariah no matter where I go within the American church.

Although I'm naturally an extrovert, I've learned how to find peace in the presence of God alone. I know how to cling to the old rugged cross. God is teaching me how to love and forgive without condition. God has allowed me to write the truth, speak the truth, and wear the truth on my chest. He has given me the confidence to say, "Black lives matter"—period, without a disclaimer, conditional clause, or defense.

Healing requires knowing what you will allow. My image-bearing identity—the unshakable Spirit at work within, the strength passed down through the blood of my ancestors, the history like the wind behind my back, the brown skin that I will not take off, the strong, kinky hair that does not submit to outside judgment or a comb—won't allow me to drink from broken cisterns anymore. Broken cisterns cannot hold the living water that brings life, hope, and healing (see Jeremiah 2:13).

Ann Voskamp declares that God is inviting us to heal: "My most meaningful calling [is] to be His healing to the hurting. My own brokenness, driving me into Christ's, is exactly where I can touch the brokenhearted. Our most meaningful purpose can be found exactly in our most painful brokenness." She's right! "We can be brokers of healing exactly where we have known the most brokenness."

Broken and healed—this is the way I offer myself up to God and to you.

LOVE REDEEMS OUR BROKENNESS

Loving yourself means being honest with God and others about your struggles. Through my wilderness experiences, I have discovered that the people I love need to see the real me with an unveiled face. They don't have to always understand, but they do need to see the glow when I experience the glory of the God, without me wondering if that brightness is going to blind them. And I need to speak honestly when that light starts to dim without wondering if the Lord has left us (see Exodus 34:29-35). We need not be afraid. God touches us in the darkness and in the light.

Transparency is healing. Being transparent is the only way we can allow others to take the redemptive journey with us. Nouwen reminds us that "laying down [our lives] means making [our] own faith and doubt, hope and despair, joy and sadness, courage and fear available to others as ways of getting in touch with the Lord of life."

Staying connected to God is something we learn to do together. We especially need this support when we have gone through a dark place, when we are taking a new journey, or when we don't know where we are going or what to do.

I remember sitting in the bed next to my husband. We were trying to rebuild a marriage that was broken. He was in counseling because he was broken, and that brokenness had caused us to break. I was in seminary and taking a course called "Managing Conflict." God knows what we need before we need it.

As part of my course requirements, I was reading Ken Sande's book *The Peacemaker: A Biblical Guide to Resolving Personal Conflict.* While reading, I was convicted of the many ways that I was broken, the ways that I had sinned against God and my husband. Truth is, I continued to pray (but not without doubt that God would fix us) because I had settled in. *This is how it's always going to be,* I thought. *I'm married and stuck.* And the worst confession that I made while sitting next to my husband that day was, "I had given up hope. I had lost trust that God would heal our marriage."

I wanted to heal and I wanted us to heal. I wanted to become a peacemaker and not a "peace faker." Yet the healing did not come for us individually or collectively until we truly confessed our sins to God and to each other, until we replaced the lies we had accepted and believed about the other with the truth of how God wants us to become his agents of grace for each other, and until we repented of the old way. Our healing began when we decided that we were not each other's enemies, but we were going to work and get better together.

I can't be a true peacemaker alone, and I could not sustain the holy ministry of marriage alone. Trusting God and going at it together relieves a lot of the burden of our brokenness, and it requires that we care for each other on the way. Henri Nouwen provides a healing and humbling note: "We are not the healers, we are not the reconcilers, we are not the givers of life. We are sinful, broken, vulnerable people who need as much care as anyone we care for. The mystery of ministry is that we have been chosen to make our own limited and very conditional love the gateway for the unlimited and unconditional love of God."

LOVE HEALS

The Greek language includes four words that denote different types of love. The word *agape* best communicates the unconditional commitment or faithful love defined in the New Testament (for example, 1 Corinthians 13). God is love (1 John 4:8, 16). Love is a sacrificial choice to lay down our selfish lives—our hopes, dreams, and desires—for the sake of another. Without the love that God represents and love that Jesus modeled, there can be no reconciliation of the broken. Learning to love well and learning to heal together brings about the reconciliation that leads to redemption.

Ken Sande reminds us that reconciliation is central to the entire gospel message: "The gospel shows us how important reconciliation is to God, which inspires us to do everything we can to repair any harm we have caused to others and to be reconciled to those we have offended." Our challenge is to do *everything* we can to repair any harm done. These corrective actions include self-care, personal reflection, and self-examination for our own healing. It also includes growing healthy relationships and telling the truth. It means that we must courageously take new steps to confess, repent, seek help, and, when appropriate, offer restitution and reparations.

The healing actions of confession and repentance must be honest and complete. An honest confession acknowledges the violations against God's standard and the harm against other people that we have caused. Repentance is changing our hearts concerning a matter and not just feeling bad about it. It means stopping our sinful behavior, turning around, and going in a different direction to follow God.

The problem in our culture, especially in the modern-day church, is that we are too quick to rush to a false sense of forgiveness without acknowledging the hurt or taking these healing actions. Demanding forgiveness without addressing the sin only reinforces bad behavior, strengthens individual heartbreak, and increases communal division. It does nothing in the pursuit of justice—and this is nothing short of spiritual abuse. We must understand that for- giveness can be delayed when pat- terns of abuse are at work, confession is incomplete, and repentance has not taken place.

The healing actions of confession and repentance must be honest and complete.

Christ makes this transformative work possible for us. Only when we follow him in humility can we consider the needs of others above our own needs. And only then can we address the consequences of restitution or reparations.

Unlike some of us, Moses understood that perpetual sin doesn't just impact individuals, but it also impacts communities for gen- erations. This is why public confession is essential. We must model and teach people how to respond in this way, as Moses did. When the Israelites sinned by worshiping the golden calf, Moses went before the Lord to repent. Moses had not built or worshiped the golden calf. He wasn't even there when the people sinned. Yet he took the sin of the people upon himself. He said, "This is a stiff- necked people," and "forgive our wickedness and our sin" (Exodus 34:9). With his confession Moses acknowledged the communal consequences of sin, and he also recognized that he was no better than the people God had called him to lead. Moses sets an example of how we can steadily take our sins before God, confess them to each other, and pray so we can all be healed (James 5:16).

Understanding the communal consequences of sin can also mo- tivate us to leverage our relationships, experiences, and knowledge for the sake of others. Moses consistently leveraged his relationship with the Lord to benefit the Israelites.

If you've come this far in our journey together in this book and you still conclude, "I wasn't there. I didn't own slaves, and I'm so glad things aren't as bad now as they were back then," then that would be a grave misjudgment. On the other hand, if you look at this landscape and conclude, "All the chips are in *their* favor. I'm only a victim, and there is nothing I can do about it," then that posture also misses the mark. Both of these conclusions too easily allow us to wash our hands of the deeply rooted issues that continue to affect us all today. Both forget that the healing power of the gospel requires that we first repent of our collective sin. Then, by God's grace, we can take right actions to determine a new way of loving and forgiving.

LOVE AND FORGIVENESS

I don't know whether Moses ever forgave the Israelites for breaking his heart, but I do know that learning to forgive is intrinsically linked to our capacity for love. When our hearts grow cold toward loving God, ourselves, or others, that's when the bitterness sets in. Bitterness is not good for us because it can easily turn into loathing. It can cause us to give up on people and quit our kingdom work.

I know that this work of reconciliation will look different for each of us. For me, it began in the professional arena when I served as the diversity outreach officer in the US Naval Academy Office of Admissions. It continued when my family and I landed in a church where we were ethnic minorities. Proximity—the desire to get close—is the reason I have invested more than a decade in local congregations that are predominantly white, even in a multiethnic church. The commitment to God's diverse church has been both a challenge and a risk my family has willingly taken for the sake of the gospel.

African American author and former professor Patricia Raybon has taken the same risk. In her acclaimed book *My First White Friend* she wrote, "That is why I teach white students. To close the distance. I want to get close enough to the people I've feared and envied and hated, because nearness has a funny way of dispelling old demons." If we are building for a new way of life, then we all need to make moves.

Nearness and proximity are the first relational steps that allow us to move toward reconciliation. I'm praying that those relational moves will also challenge us to act justly and address the communal sin that's evident in our nation's systemic injustices. Without intentional and consistent action, the church lacks credibility on this topic. Conversations about racial reconciliation that exclude actionable steps toward racial justice fall short of God's kingdom mission.

Being in the minority is not a normal experience for white people in the United States, but taking the lower position or positioning oneself as a minority in a certain space can go a long way in the healing, reconciliation, or redemptive process. We all have much to learn. I am committed to ministering the gospel's message of reconciliation as central to our discipleship. Laboring in this effort improves our faithful witness in a diverse and pluralistic society.

I've learned that extending forgiveness requires that I remain close to white people. I don't just mean being polite, politically correct, or tolerant. I mean being my full self in the presence of white folk—being a friend, a peacemaker, a truth teller, and a bridge builder while challenging each of us to love well, consider the other as we all grow in knowledge, and pursue higher standards for right speech and right action. We all need to get closer.

Nearness. Learning from each other. Mutual blessing—this is the reason God called the Israelites to share his commandments with all who were living among them, regardless of their ethnic heritage or economic class. Taking these steps will not always be easy, but our healing depends on it.

Living healed and whole includes regularly inviting people to get and stay on the long redemptive road, while being mindful of our temptation to quit. In spite of small wins, strokes of ego, and the need for accomplishment, quitting is an ever-present temptation. We don't want to quit, but the desire creeps in slowly when our love tank is deficient—when we are leading a stiff-necked people who don't have an eye for God's vision, when the team is grumbling, when those you are called to serve don't appreciate your sacrifices, and when the work gets too hard or too tedious. Reggie McNeal warns, "Spiritual leaders who quit loving quit leading." The enemy tries to destroy us and the work God has assigned to us by tempting us to quit loving. The lack of love contributes to the lack of relationship and the lack of godly leadership.

Please don't quit. The kingdom is among you, and the kingdom is within you (Luke 17:20-21). It is within our reach to experience, embody, and participate in God's kingdom *now*. Yet we know that we will *not yet* experience the full blessing and benefits of the kingdom until Christ's return. We are part of God's redemptive story, and in that story we are drawn to move closer to God, closer to our authentic selves, and closer to others.

TRUTH IS: Healing requires our movement toward God, our authentic lives, and others. Making this move helps us love well, and it guards our hearts against bitterness.

REFLECTION QUESTION: What are some practical ways you can delight in self-care, and ways you can move closer to others who are different?

SCRIPTURE MEDITATION:

> In your unfailing love you will lead
>> the people you have redeemed.
> In your strength you will guide them
>> to your holy dwelling. (Exodus 15:13)

PERSONAL AFFIRMATION: God is love. His healing power covers and sustains me on my redemptive journey.

CALL TO ACTION: Are you tired, burdened, weary, or heavy laden? Go to the spa. Take a walk or a nap; take a break. What are your tangible opportunities for self-care and healing? Who can keep you accountable for these actions until they become habits?

PRAYER: Lord, thank you for restoring my soul and leading me in the path of righteousness (Psalm 23:3). Amen.

TWEET: Learning to love well and learning to heal together brings about the reconciliation that leads to redemption. @asistasjourney #ASojournersTruth

 LIGHT

TRUTH IS, BEAUTY CAN COME FROM ASHES

For the first time I realized that my life was just
full of brokenness. . . . I do what I do because I'm
broken too. . . . We are all broken by something.
. . . Our shared brokenness [connects] us.

BRYAN STEVENSON, *JUST MERCY*

*D*o you regret that you were not there when your mother died?"
he asked.

My spiritual director was not pulling any punches that day. It was more than seventeen years after my mother's death, and it was the first time I allowed myself to enter into deep conversation about it. He knew I was a mess and he was going for broke—not looking to break me down, but perhaps hoping for a breakthrough that would offer some relief.

I promptly responded, "No. I didn't want to see my mother quit on life."

Let me be crystal clear: my mother was no quitter! She was just broken and tired—and yes, there is a difference.

As I looked at my spiritual director through the video session on my computer screen, I had a humble appreciation for his presence in my life. People don't always ask deep or thought-provoking questions, nor do we listen well when they do. I was thankful that on this day he acted as a shepherd guiding me to remember the broken places I sometimes try to forget. He reminded me of things that I desperately need to remember because they make me who I am.

Remembering shows me that I am still broken by the grief in the now, yet I am and will always be Sallie's daughter in the not-yet kingdom. I look forward to the day when my mother and I are reconnected, neither broken anymore. So I shared my brokenness, naming the shock, awe, and emptiness of losing the most important person in my life.

She was the one who first taught me the truth about this world, about God, and about myself. She was the one who lived through and shared the stories of world-changing civil rights leaders such as Rosa, Malcolm, Fannie, and of course, MLK.

THE MOUNTAINTOP

There isn't an American who doesn't know, love, or occasionally quote Dr. Martin Luther King Jr.'s "I Have a Dream" speech. Whenever I visit the nation's capital and walk the Washington Mall, I imagine what joining in that experience must have felt like. Dr. King stood on the steps of the Lincoln Memorial and delivered an impassioned speech to a crowd of some 250,000 people, and the glory of the Lord descended on them. He had a redemptive vision, a dream for all children, for our country, and for a more just and loving world. I love that speech!

However, when we separate that inspirational speech from King's selfless commitment to justice, economic empowerment, advocacy, selfless sacrifice, or Christian ministry, we lose sight of the big picture of his life's work and calling. Dr. King was a preacher who got a glimpse of God's new kingdom, and he actively pursued it. At every turn, he stood behind Jesus and on the side of the little person—the poor, the oppressed, and the marginalized. When his earthly work was done, God called him to his eternal home.

It is in the words of his final speech, not his dream, that you get the true essence of this leader's purpose. That is why "I've Been to the Mountaintop" is my all-time favorite of his speeches. It's the one that reveals his brokenness and shows his unwavering commitment to love and justice. This speech displays the shepherd's sacrifice for his people to the very end. It's the one I revisit when my heart and mind get weary on this redemptive journey.

Brother Martin delivered this famous speech (and if you haven't read it, you need to put this book down right now and do so) in Memphis, Tennessee, at the Bishop Charles Mason Temple Church of God in Christ to an audience of eleven thousand people on the night before his assassination. His friends reported that he was sick—feverish, fighting a cold, and depressed. The work of righteousness, reconciliation, and redemption can be hard on the mind, body, and spirit. He didn't use any notes; he just spoke from the heart as his pure, authentic, and broken self. His soul was weary.

Not only was he a man acquainted with sorrow, he was also a man frequently aware of the fragilities of life and of his impending death. He got stabbed at the age of twenty-nine, and his dear friend Andrew Young wrote that King "often discussed this near-death experience to remind his followers that death was an ever-present possibility. He usually did so in a rather joking manner, concluding for us that we had better be ready to die."

The mountaintop speech was part of an advocacy campaign for poor and underpaid sanitation workers who were on strike. King put the struggle of these few within the context of the bigger picture and survival of the entire community. Their business was not just survival. Their pursuit was a human rights revolution. He acknowledged, "If something isn't done and done in a hurry to bring the colored peoples of the world out of their long years of poverty, their long years of hurt and neglect, the whole world is doomed." Although the work was hard, he was happy about this redemptive movement. This revolution—this fight for the sacredness, dignity, deliverance, and freedom of all lives—is the mission for which we have all been drafted.

This fiery preacher spoke from the heart about the great journey that Moses made with his people:

> If I were standing at the beginning of time with the possibility of taking a kind of general and panoramic view of the whole of human history up to now, and the Almighty said to me, "Martin Luther King, which age would you like to live in?" I would take my mental flight by Egypt, and I would watch God's children in their magnificent trek from the dark dungeons of Egypt through, or rather, across the Red Sea, through the wilderness, on toward the Promised Land. And in spite of its magnificence I wouldn't stop there. . . .
>
> Strangely enough, I would turn to the Almighty and say, "If you allow me to live just a few years in the second half of the twentieth century, I will be happy."
>
> Now that's a strange statement to make because the world is all messed up. . . . But I know, somehow, that only when it is dark enough can you see the stars.

Brother Martin told the people that he was happy to live in a messed-up period in history because only in the darkness is God's beautiful light revealed. In this *kairos* moment, Dr. King embodies the words of the apostle Paul: "For Christ's sake, I delight in weaknesses, in insults, in hardships, in persecutions, in difficulties" (2 Corinthians 12:10).

Then Dr. King closed the speech by calling his people to stick together because their work was not yet done. When there is unfinished business, each of us must tend to our own work with an unwavering commitment to God's kingdom vision. Our kingdom work requires collaboration and the pursuit of good for the whole community. We must all put our hands to the plow and not look back, and we must stick together. Dr. King informs us:

> Whenever Pharaoh wanted to prolong the period of slavery of Egypt, he had a favorite, favorite formula for doing it. What was that? He kept the slaves fighting among themselves. But whenever the slaves get together, something happens in Pharaoh's court, and he cannot hold the slaves in slavery. When the slaves get together, that's the beginning of getting out of slavery. Now let us maintain unity.

Redemption means unity in God's kingdom. United we stand! Regardless of what happens or who we lose along the way, we must collectively persevere to the end. This requires an unselfishness, a Christlike laying down of our lives and sacrifice for the sake of other people.

The temptation of the enemy is to cause us to delight in our individual progress. It's far too easy for us to get comfortable, to celebrate, and to pat ourselves on the back because of our own personal success when the systems are still failing our communities. Sometimes we have to lose individually so we can win collectively. The words of Brother Martin present a redemptive challenge. Fight until the end! Show up for one another. "Be concerned about your brother [and sister]." We will rise or fall together. We must finish our redemptive work!

We must collectively persevere to the end.

We now find ourselves in the twenty-first century, and the world is still messed up. We are all broken, yet we can hold fast to Dr. King's words of wisdom and the lessons learned from the prophet Moses. We, who have come up out of slavery to survive the wilderness, can enter the Promised Land.

A MOUNTAINTOP EXPERIENCE

For all of his standing against injustice, his devotion to God, and his service rendered on behalf of the people, Moses knew that he would not see the Promised Land. Because of his faithful communion with God, Moses continued to live and work in spite of his shattered dreams and expectations. Moses walked in his purpose even when his own people slandered his name or tried to murder him on numerous occasions. He led in spite of their ungratefulness or lack of faith.

At the end of Moses' journey, it was just him and the Lord. Moses climbed Mount Nebo, where God showed him the whole land he had promised to give to Abraham's descendants (Deuteronomy 34:1-4). The Israelites were going into battle, and their fearless leader must have been filled with both concern and regret. I imagine Moses shedding tears of joy and disappointment. At 120 years old, his body was physically strong, but he was no longer able to lead them (Deuteronomy 34:5-7). His work was finished. His life's purpose was fulfilled. He died on that mountaintop.

Death comes for all of us, and indeed it is an able teacher. The reality of our impending death teaches us to stay ready, to stay in the fight, and to live purposeful lives every day no matter the cost. It reminds us that there is a higher calling for our brokenness, our struggles, and our work. Our daily business can't be all about us. We need to remain humble and intentionally raise up the next generation of leaders to carry on the work that we began. Death informs us that at some point, we all need to let go.

Moses did not enter the Promised Land, but he did enter the presence of God and found rest for his weary soul.

ASHES TO ASHES

We all have to wrestle with the shaping elements, the history, and the wilderness experiences that change our lives forever. The people, the places, and the pain we encounter all guide us into our life's purpose. The miracle of God's sovereignty and grace is that he knows all things and he doesn't waste anything. Whatever God has assigned or allowed in your life is not to break you down but rather to build you up with a renewed heart, mind, and vision for living life in his kingdom. Death always comes before resurrection; ashes precede the beauty.

I've suffered through many deaths. The truth is, my soul has been far too weary for such a young traveler. It was on a day when I was struggling to see the light that my spiritual director asked about my mother's death. I told him the story.

It was a cold, dark winter night, and the company chief awakened me in the wee hours of the morning at the Naval Academy. He was the messenger who delivered the news

> The people, the places, and the pain we encounter all guide us into our life's purpose.

that death had knocked on my mother's door. The word *no* escaped my lips multiple times. This cannot be real; somebody wake me from this nightmare. Please. But I was awake.

The rabbi on duty was called to comfort me. This stranger sat with his hand pressed firmly on my shoulder as I lay feeble on the couch in the chief's office. I cried until I had no more tears.

When I returned home, my grief-stricken father stared out the window in shock, and he barely ate or spoke a word for three whole days. There was a funeral to plan, and I was the matriarch now. It was my turn to bring everyone together, to comfort the family, including my sister and our little brother, who didn't fully understand that his momma wasn't coming back home. Now was the time to honor and celebrate our fallen giant, so we sat together in a dimly lit funeral parlor to make the arrangements. We, her children, selected a tribute.

Her work was done, and yet there remained unfinished business. There are appropriate times to consider all of the people and experiences that have formed us into who we are today. There is a time to consider our history. There is a time to grieve our losses, and there is a time to renew ourselves, strengthen our backs, and rededicate our lives.

I said to my spiritual director, "My mother went exactly how she wanted to go." Like Brother Martin, who regularly spoke of his impending death, or Moses, who informed the people that he would not continue with them into the Promised Land, she gave us all fair warning that her appointed time was near. We just chose not to see the signs.

Only weeks before her death, she told me, "You know, Tasha, when I had my first aneurism, I said to the Lord that if he would just allow me to see my children grow up, I would be grateful."

I had been a small child when she went off to Texas for her first open heart surgery. My sister and I stayed with our grandparents for weeks until my mother returned to us, fragile and with no voice to speak for days. After briefly recalling that experience, I gazed into her eyes and said, "Momma, we're grown now." She smiled slightly, patted my hand, and said, "I know."

During one of our last phone conversations, I asked her directly, "Momma, do you want me to come home for your surgery?" She quickly replied, "No, baby. Stay right there and focus on the work you have to do." It was the week before my final exams at the Naval Academy.

My father relayed her final moments to me: "Sal had me go down the hall and ask the nurse to bring some ice because her throat was dry. I don't know why she didn't buzz the nurse from her bedside like she'd always done. When I came back, she was gone."

As I reflect on these sacred moments, I am often reminded of these words of Martin Luther King Jr.: "I just want to do God's will. And He's allowed me to go up to the mountain. And I've looked over, and I've seen the Promised Land. I may not get there with you. But I want you to know tonight that we, as a people, will get to the Promised Land."

My Moses was dead. The eternal kingdom was before her, and she longed for this world no more. There on a hospital bed in Columbia, South Carolina, she laid all of her brokenness and burdens down. On December 9, 1999—only two days after her fifty-second birthday—her earthly journey came to an end and she entered into God's eternal light.

She was not alone in that sick room, just as Brother Martin was not alone on that ledge where he was shot down like a helpless deer, and Moses was not alone on that mountaintop. Each of these took their last breath just as they had taken their first: in the presence of God. Rabbi Abraham Heschel wrote, "For the pious person, it is a privilege to die."

LIGHT IN THE DARKNESS

It is a good thing to contemplate the end of one's life. Pondering the end challenges us to consider the role God has called us to play in his great redemption story. It makes us think about the obituary we want written. What tribute will your children and those you influence share about you? Whether or not we allow God to shift our allegiances, priorities, choices, and commitments can radically change lives, communities, churches, and the future. This is how history is shaped and legacies are formed.

I speak of a spiritual legacy in the same manner that the writer of Hebrews documented the names of so many ordinary people who acted in faith (Hebrews 11). You too can be counted among the faithful! You can respond to the darkness of this world as one who preaches good news to the poor, binds up the brokenhearted, proclaims freedom for the captives, releases prisoners from darkness, comforts those who mourn, and provides for those who grieve (Isaiah 61:1-3). Because Christ has come and because the Holy Spirit of God is at work in and through you, you can bestow on broken humans "a crown of beauty instead of ashes, the oil of joy instead of mourning, and a garment of praise instead of a spirit of despair" (Isaiah 61:3).

Our physical death can transport us into the eternal beauty of God's great light. And only the eternal, glorious light puts to death the darkness of this world.

TRUTH IS: We are all broken people, and death will come for all of us. In our brokenness we learn that the beauty of God's light overcomes the world's darkness.

REFLECTION QUESTION: Consider the names and faithful witnesses of the people listed in Hebrews 11. Who are the people that have modeled God's faithfulness throughout your life?

SCRIPTURE MEDITATION: "I have fought the good fight, I have finished the race, I have kept the faith. Now there is in store for me the crown of righteousness, which the Lord, the righteous Judge, will award to me on that day—and not only to me, but also to all who have longed for his appearing" (2 Timothy 4:7-8).

PERSONAL AFFIRMATION: God will finish what he started; therefore, I will faithfully join his redemptive work.

CALL TO ACTION: How can you honor the Moses figures in your life while they are among the land of the living?

PRAYER: God, there is so much brokenness, so many hurts, disappointments, losses, and missed opportunities, which cause us to lose sight of you in this world. Help our grieving hearts. Have mercy on us sinners, and make us faithful stewards of the passions, gifts, and calling you have placed within and before us. Make us steadfast until the very end. In Jesus' name, Amen.

TWEET: Only the eternal, glorious light puts to death the darkness of this world. @asistasjourney #ASojournersTruth

CHAPTER SIXTEEN

TRUTH IS, WE NEED COURAGE
TO LIVE REDEEMED

The conquering lion
Shall break every chain
Give him the victory
Again and again and again and again.

LAURYN HILL, "THE CONQUERING LION"

O ur bags neatly lined the wall of the foyer. Our eyes could barely meet each other's. There was a mix of overwhelming peace and grief among us. Our hearts were now divided between a continent, a country, and a people that we had grown to love and the continent, the country, and the people that we dearly missed and were returning to back home.

Caught up in my emotions, I brushed pass the other women—these beautiful, African American women who accompanied me on the trip to Kigali, Rwanda, many of us visiting the continent of Africa for the first time—as Pastor Fred Isaac Katagwa, executive director of Africa New Life, gathered us for our final time of reflection and prayer. "I want to thank you," he said. "This is the first time we have done anything like this."

We reminded him how important it was for us to come—not as missionaries with a posture of colonialism that is often associated with travelers from the West, but as learners, equals, loving family members in the kingdom, and participants in the great global work God is doing in the world. He thanked us for not forgetting about the women, as Western missionaries frequently come to spend time with the children. Very few come to teach, encourage, or financially support the impoverished and often forgotten women, many of whom are widows and mothers. We told him about the special bond that had formed between our team and the women of Rwanda, and the redemptive thread we experienced through the telling of stories, the sharing of work and life, the breaking of bread, and the opening of God's Word together.

Then we all stood, and Pastor Katagwa began to boldly pray for us: "God, I thank you that although their ancestors were taken away from this continent in chains, you have brought them back home, and you have brought them back free!" I exhaled long. I clasped their hands. The tears flowed.

This is what redemption feels like: an anointed prayer, supportive hands to hold, a circle of trust, a deep breath of health, knowing that you are loved and not forgotten, and the freedom to go to your defined home. Redemption is God's grace to us. Graciously I had received it in the wilderness, and graciously I would courageously share it.

GOD'S GRACE SUSTAINS THE COURAGEOUS ONES

"Moses my servant is dead" (Joshua 1:2). I imagine this statement was the source of much grief for Joshua as he considered the weight of the leadership challenge set before him. He had survived the wilderness, and now he had to pick up the mantle to lead like Moses. Joshua would rescue the people from their impending death and usher them into the Promised Land. Now was the time to move out! God commanded him:

> Be strong and courageous, because you will lead these people
> to inherit the land I swore to their ancestors to give them.

> Be strong and very courageous. Be careful to obey all the law my servant Moses gave you; do not turn from it to the right or to the left, that you may be successful wherever you go. . . . Have I not commanded you? Be strong and courageous. Do not be afraid; do not be discouraged, for the LORD your God will be with you wherever you go. (Joshua 1:6-7, 9).

Three times God told Joshua that strength and courage were needed for the way ahead. The Israelites were about to go places and do things they had never done before.

They were entering new territory, and God revealed the critical spiritual elements that were required for charting the way. The officers (the military commanders who were in the struggle with the people) told the Israelites: "When you see the ark of the covenant of the LORD your God, and the Levitical priests carrying it, you are to move out from your positions and follow it. Then you will know which way to go, since you have never been this way before" (Joshua 3:3-4).

They had to get behind God because they didn't know where they were going. The ark helped them to remember all of the things God had accomplished for them. It contained the Ten Commandments (God's Word), a jar of manna (reminding them of how God fed and sustained them in the wilderness), and Aaron's budded staff (signifying the importance of letting God, not the people, choose the spiritual leaders who would represent him; Numbers 17:1-11; Hebrews 9:4). The strategy for the new world required them to remember God's Word, remember who God was and what God had done, and follow God's appointed leadership. They had to move with the intention of following God in the same way they had followed him in the cloud and fire on their journey out of their old home and through the wilderness.

COURAGE FOR DEEP CHANGE

Being at a crossroads provides wonderful opportunities for courageous action. At the crossroads we decide whether we will follow the steps of the generation of Israelites who constantly looked back at their old home in Egypt to declare its greatness instead of actively preparing for their new home in the Promised Land. The entire exodus journey was the community's invitation to deep change, and change eventually took place. Moses was changed. Joshua was changed.

If we truly want to effect change, then we must first allow ourselves to experience change. Maybe following God wholeheartedly doesn't trouble us, but making the commitment to deep change is what's so frightening. Far too often we fear what we will lose instead of considering what might be gained if we take the courageous journey to change.

> If we truly want to effect change, then we must first allow ourselves to experience change.

When Mahatma Gandhi said, "Be the change you wish to see in the world," he was calling people to deep change. When Fannie Lou Hamer said, "When I liberate others, I liberate myself," she was calling people to deep change. Whenever Dr. King spoke, he most certainly was calling people to change. He said that transformed people needed to cease imitating and begin innovating because innovation is necessary if you are building a new way. We need to reject complacency and continuously create ways to challenge the consciousness of our nation and establish a new cultural climate.

Courageous actions and creatively initiating real change can benefit the entire nation and shape the future leaders of our world. Do you have the courage to do the hard thing? Don't be timid. Go for it!

Often I tell my mentees that life is not about how you start, it's about how you finish. We can craft a better future. We can commit to experiencing the presence of God's kingdom on earth as it is in heaven. We can become the type of people who get behind God and move courageously even when we don't know where we are going. We can be the redeemed who build for a new day. We can be disciples who make disciples, mentors who multiply, leaders, servants, and laborers who seize the opportunity to lay critical building blocks for the new kingdom.

Truth is, you need to know your foundation, understand your history, reflect on your wilderness experiences, and courageously walk in your redemption. Who are you? What do you value? What do you expect out of this life? The time has passed for pa-tiently waiting for change that has not come. The time has passed for waiting for a seat at the table, waiting for others to acknowledge your voice, waiting for the power of the vote or the change in your community. Now is the time to build new systems and to host equitable tables. How will you contribute?

> The time has passed for patiently waiting for change that has not come.

A NEW HOME

You build a house. You nurture a home. Luther Vandross's classic song "A House Is Not a Home" comes to mind. He sings that furniture and rooms don't make a home because he's not meant to live alone. When I think about the courageous actions needed to intentionally nurture a home, I'm reminded of God's belief that it is not good for humans to be alone (Genesis 2:18). As I work for my nonprofit, this simple understanding reinforces the importance of one of our core values—network.

At a Missio Alliance consultation event, I was privileged to hear Tom Lin, president of InterVarsity Christian Fellowship, give a presentation about the missional challenges and opportunities we are facing in the United States and the types of partnerships we need to build as a result. Tom indicated that what we need now is collaboration of leadership focused on the mission. He challenged us to consider uncommon collaborations and said we need resilience and the ability to risk our reputations when taking a stand. He stated that we need more brothers and sisters of color in leadership. He reminded us of the importance of having people commit to working in the trenches; everyone can't be out front. Finally, he stated that we need accurate data collection for informed leadership. Tom was teaching us how to build and nurture an informed, engaged, and diverse network in God's kingdom.

The issues we have pondered in this book are not just black and white concerns. Pain, consciousness, physical and spiritual deaths, and the ways we build are nothing short of missional issues. We cannot lead with integrity or make disciples of all nations if our loyalties are divided between our old home—the kingdom of this world—and our new one—the kingdom where God reigns supreme. We cannot become a people of God from every tribe, language, and nation if we only listen to, read, or accept the leadership of white men.

God has said of his new kingdom,

> In the last days . . .
>   I will pour out my Spirit on all people.
> Your sons and daughters will prophesy,
>   your young men will see visions,
>   your old men will dream dreams.
> Even on my servants, both men and women,
>   I will pour out my Spirit in those days,
>   and they will prophesy. (Acts 2:17-18, quoting Joel 2:28-29)

We need to prepare and condition people to hear prophetic
words from all the daughters
and sons, young and old, who
have the Spirit of God. We
need to take the courageous

> We need to take the courageous steps to listen to the right people and chart a new way ahead.

steps to listen to the right people and chart a new way ahead.

CHOOSING THE PATH OF LIFE

The story of Joshua leading God's people into a new land has sim-
ilarities to the life of King Solomon. With his parting words (Deuteronomy 31:1-8), Moses prepared Joshua for leadership in the
same way that King David prepared his son Solomon for kingship
(1 Kings 2:1-12). Both of these young men had opportunities to
watch and obey the Lord. When their mentors departed, Joshua
courageously obeyed what he was taught until the very end.
Solomon ultimately did not.

The hearts of fallen humans are rebellious. Even when God has
guided us so clearly and provided a new way for us to live victorious
and free, we are prone to reject his ways and sin. We do have a
choice in these matters. Some will choose to follow in the footsteps
of Joshua and others in the footsteps of Solomon. Some will follow
in the ways of Abel and others in the ways of Cain. Some will take
the risk of making a long journey to undergo real life transformation like Ruth, while others will simply return to the comforts
of their old homes like Orpah (Ruth 1:6-18). Some will follow
Christ the resurrected King and find new life, while others will
follow the prince of this world, which leads to death (John 12:28-32;
14:30-31). It is sad that in life, ministry, and work so many people
"tend to choose slow death over deep change."

We must not forget the words God has spoken. Moses told the
people, "Take to heart all the words I have solemnly declared to

you this day, so that you may command your children to obey carefully all the words of this law. They are not just idle words for you—they are your life" (Deuteronomy 32:46-47). Joshua also reminded them of the importance of God's Word through covenant renewal ceremonies. Covenant renewals required God's people to look back and remember how far God had brought them. They encouraged the people to recommit themselves to following the Lord wholeheartedly. When the children heard these renewals, the commitment crossed over generations.

Covenant renewals always gave the people a choice: "Now fear the Lord and serve him with all faithfulness. . . . But if serving the Lord seems undesirable to you, then choose for yourselves this day whom you will serve. . . . But as for me and my household, we will serve the Lord" (Joshua 24:14-15). Build a house. Nurture a home. Remember God's words: "Impress them on your children. Talk about them when you sit at home and when you walk along the road, when you lie down and when you get up. Tie them as symbols on your hands and bind them on your foreheads. Write them on the doorframes of your houses and on your gates" (Deuteronomy 6:7-9). Choose this day whom you will serve! If serving the Lord seems pleasing to you, then remember, walk in obedience, and set up memorial stones.

Every day we can make a choice for covenant renewal—to remember God's Word, to remember who God is and what he has done, and to recommit ourselves to wholeheartedly following him.

My experience in Rwanda was a covenant renewal. A few short weeks later, I found myself staring out at the crashing waves of the Atlantic Ocean from the shores of Lagos, Nigeria. I had just finished a walk I'd never considered making—along the same path my ancestors were forced to take when they were bound and chained for enslavement. The sky was clear. The air was crisp. The wind blew forcefully as I made the long trek along the Badagry Slave Route, also called the "Point of No Return" or the "Journey to Unknown Destination."

As I stared at the water, Pastor Fred's words rang in my ears. I whispered into the air, "God, I thank you that although my ancestors were taken away from this continent in chains, you have brought me back home, and I am free! I am no longer bound by the chains of sin and death. I do not fear what any human being can do to me" (see Romans 8:1-2; Matthew 10:28).

I realized in that moment that in spite of my surroundings, I could live redeemed; that I could choose life every day; that I could make my home because Jesus, the great redeemer, is ever present with me wherever I go (Psalm 139:8). I realized that there was nothing holding me back. I could walk, run, or swim in that moment. My hope had been restored, my strength had been renewed, and indeed, I believed I could fly (Isaiah 40:29-31).

The chains are broken!

The chains are broken!

The chains are broken!

I am free!

I need only the strength and courage to continue on the path and to tell the truth. So I turned around and began the long walk toward home.

TRUTH IS: We all need courage to act, change, live, and stay on the redemptive path.

REFLECTION QUESTION: How is God inviting you into deep, courageous change?

SCRIPTURE MEDITATION:

> Rend your heart
>   and not your garments.
> Return to the Lord your God,
>   for he is gracious and compassionate,
> slow to anger and abounding in love,
>   and he relents from sending calamity. (Joel 2:13)

PERSONAL AFFIRMATION: I am committed to making the change that leads to life.

CALL TO ACTION: You go now in freedom to learn, to know, to speak, and to courageously live the truth.

PRAYER: God, I thank you that you do not treat us as our sins deserve. You are gracious and just, slow to anger, and abounding in mercy. Thank you for inviting us to deep change. Thank you for the Holy Spirit, who allows me to change. Give me a willing heart to change for the sake of loving you and loving other people. Give me courage and strength for the journey. Make me your agent of goodness in the world. Amen.

TWEET: Being at a crossroads provides wonderful opportunities for courageous action. @asistasjourney #ASojournersTruth

BENEDICTION

In your unfailing love you will lead
the people you have redeemed.
In your strength you will guide them
to your holy dwelling.

EXODUS 15:13

Amen.

ACKNOWLEDGMENTS

I did not see this book coming. I was working on another book idea when this one started keeping me up at night. It made me look deeper and then turn away and look again at the God who spoke through the burning bush. It has been hard. I could not have weathered the emotional and spiritual storm without the early readers who made me go back to rework it, to connect the dots, to clarify the message. Many thanks to my dear friends and early readers: Jada Johnson, Natalie Stennis, Deronta Robinson, Pamela Rossi-Keen, and Stefini Greer.

I thank God for a prayer team who understands the real battle and are willing to fight for me, my family, and the ministry work that God has assigned to my hands.

Thank God for the privilege of going to the continent of Africa. I simply would not have been able to complete this work without the message of humility, healing, and hope that God ministered to my spirit in Rwanda. I am especially grateful for my #W2WRwanda sisters: Carline Adams, Delina McPhall, Faitth Brooks, Latasha Morrison, Latoya Collins-Jones, and Stephanie Ivery; for the mighty praying mothers of our tribe, Mom Jeanne Brown, Francine Pierson, and Susan Seay; and to Amena Brown Owen for extending the invitation to me. Keep on singing, praying, laughing, and loving, sistas! Amena, thank you for all the girl talks, the wordsmithing, the watchful eyes, the tea, the mentorship, and for giving me the courage to trust my own instincts.

Soong-Chan Rah, thank you for taking a look at the first draft of the book proposal and telling me to go with it! Jo Saxton, you are always ready with an encouraging word, wisdom, and support. God bless you, sis.

Thank you to the mothers: Mary Thompson, Lula Loynes, Loretta Mack, Linda Jones, and Joyce Garrett, for helping me know God and myself, and for teaching me how to choose well. Thank you to my family and the Orangeburg community for raising me.

Special thanks to the whole IVP team, including Cindy Bunch, Elissa Schauer, and Helen Lee. We did it!

To my literary agent, Tim Beals of Credo Communications, your advocacy for my voice, ministry, and work means everything. I am so glad that we found each other at the right time and that we are in this together.

To Mrs. Patricia Raybon, thank you for continuing to say, "Yes," when I call on you, and for being an example I am honored to follow.

To the founding board members of Leadership LINKS, Inc., you are my family. At times you are Miriam, Aaron, Hur, Jethro, or Joshua. God knows you and has rightfully positioned you for what you need to be and when. May I be the same anchor of love, accountability, and support for you. For the brave new director, Graham, our advisors, and our volunteers, thank you for believing. To the parents, thank you for trusting. To the LINKS Leaders, remember who we are together!

Ashley, you are my sunshine, humility, and joy on many days. I love you, girl. Deronta, you are the love of my life. Thank you for taking the journey. Thank you, God, for being near and trusting me to deliver this message. It's yours.

For the King and his kingdom,
Natasha

NOTES

FOREWORD

1 *There's no agony like*: Zora Neale Hurston, *Dust Tracks on a Road: An Autobiography* (New York: HarperPerennial, 1996), 176.

they're often wrongly attributed: Erin McKean, "The Wise Words of Maya Angelou. Or Someone, Anyway," *New York Times*, April 9, 2015, www.nytimes.com/2015/04/10/opinion/the-wise-words-of-maya -angelou-or-someone-anyway.html.

in a society: James H. Cone, *The Cross and the Lynching Tree* (Maryknoll, NY: Orbis Books, 2011), xvi.

If I didn't define myself for myself: Audre Lorde, "Learning from the 60s," in *Sister Outsider: Essays and Speeches* (New York: Crossing Press/ Ten Speed Press, 2007), 137.

2 *Negro poverty*: Lyndon B. Johnson, "Commencement Address at Howard University: 'To Fulfill These Rights,'" June 4, 1965, www.presidency.ucsb .edu/ws/?pid=27021.

PREFACE

4 *This biblical narrative has had*: Richard A. Horsley, *Jesus and Empire: The Kingdom of God and the New World Disorder* (Minneapolis: Augsburg Fortress, 2003), 1-2.

1 PAIN

10 *New Orleans invented the brown paper bag party*: Michael Dyson, *Come Hell or High Water: Hurricane Katrina and the Color of Disaster* (New York: Basic Civitas, 2006), 150-51.

11 *When one person hurts*: Ann Voskamp, *The Broken Way: A Daring Path into the Abundant Life* (Grand Rapids: Zondervan, 2016), 28.

13 *Perhaps nowhere in society*: Chanequa Walker-Barnes, *Too Heavy a Yoke: Black Women and the Burden of Strength* (Eugene, OR: Cascade, 2014), 5.

14 *The heart dies a slow death*: This is a quote from the film *Memoirs of a Geisha*, directed by Rob Marshall, screenplay by Robin Swicord (Columbia Pictures, 2005).

17   *I've got so much*: Kurt Carr, "For Every Mountain," *No One Else* (Gospocentric, 1998).

20   *Not one thing in your life*: Voskamp, *Broken Way*, 12.

2 GRACE

24   *[She] is the woman who constantly*: Chanequa Walker-Barnes, *Too Heavy a Yoke: Black Women and the Burden of Strength* (Eugene, OR: Cascade, 2014), 4.

     What we truly admire: Andy Crouch, *Strong and Weak: Embracing a Life of Love, Risk, and True Flourishing* (Downers Grove, IL: InterVarsity Press, 2016), 47.

3 COMMUNITY

31   *Leaders are not shaped in isolation*: Reggie McNeal, *A Work of Heart: Understanding How God Shapes Spiritual Leaders* (San Francisco: Jossey-Bass, 2011), 115.

32   *Sing a song full of the faith*: James Weldon Johnson, "The Black National Anthem," or "Lift Every Voice and Sing," 1900, BlackHistory.com, http://blackhistory.com/content/62362/the-black-national-anthem.

36   *the Great Migration*: See Isabel Wilkerson, *The Warmth of Other Suns: The Epic Story of America's Great Migration* (New York: Vintage Books, 2010), back cover.

38   *leaders are not shaped*: McNeal, *Work of Heart*, 115.

39   *God of our weary years*: Johnson, "Lift Every Voice and Sing."

4 PURPOSE

43   *Plebes were defined*: United States Naval Academy, *Reef Points 1998–1999* (Annapolis, MD: United States Naval Academy), 222.

45   *designed to facilitate an understanding*: United States Naval Academy, *Reef Points 1998–1999*, 179.

51   *Sometimes we are not present*: Natasha Sistrunk Robinson, *Mentor for Life: Finding Purpose Through Intentional Discipleship* (Grand Rapids: Zondervan, 2016), 86.

52   *the bitter hours when we discovered*: Margaret Walker, "For My People," in *The Vintage Book of African American Poetry: 200 Years of Vision, Struggle, Power, Beauty, and Triumph from 50 Outstanding Poets*, ed. Michael S. Harper and Anthony Walton (New York: Vintage Books, 2000), 177.

PART TWO: HISTORY

55 *The biblical exodus narrative has given*: Donald T. Phillips, *Martin Luther King, Jr. on Leadership: Inspiration & Wisdom for Challenging Times* (New York: Warner Books, 1999), 63.

5 CONSCIOUSNESS

58 *What began as nonviolent protests*: Jack Bass and Jack Nelson, *The Orangeburg Massacre* (Macon, GA: Mercer University Press, 1996), 58, 72, 75-76.

59 *On February 28, 1968*: Bass and Nelson, *Orangeburg Massacre*, 65.

This massacre was the first of its kind: Jack Bass, "Orangeburg Massacre," in *South Carolina Encyclopedia*, updated October 21, 2016, www.scencyclopedia.org/sce/entries/orangeburg-massacre.

Orangeburg students who began protesting: Dale Linder-Altman, "Students Faced Water Hoses, Arrest in Downtown Orangeburg," *Times and Democrat*, March 15, 2010, http://thetandd.com/news/students -faced-water-hoses-arrest-in-downtown-orangeburg/article_2f6b56ba -6f1e-53ab-b6b3-12be0efa1d14.html.

61 *Martin's voice was more*: Andrew Young, introduction to *A Call to Conscience: The Landmark Speeches of Dr. Martin Luther King, Jr.*, ed. Clayborne Carson and Kris Shepard (New York: Warner Books, 2001), vii-viii.

62 *The bottom line for leaders*: Edgar H. Schein, *Organizational Culture and Leadership*, 4th ed. (San Francisco: Jossey-Bass, 2010), 22.

What is going on here?: Schein, *Organizational Culture and Leadership*, 320.

63 *the loss of millions of tourism dollars*: Kriston Capps, "The Confederate Flag Has Cost South Carolina Millions in Tourism," CityLab, June 24, 2015, www.citylab.com/life/2015/06/the-confederate-flag-has -cost-south-carolina-millions-in-tourism/396566.

the Confederate flag continued to fly: Stephanie McCrummen and Elahe Izadi, "Confederate Flag Comes Down on South Carolina's Statehouse Grounds," *Washington Post*, July 10, 2015, www.washingtonpost .com/news/post-nation/wp/2015/07/10/watch-live-as-the-confederate -flag-comes-down-in-south-carolina/?utm_term=.a7471f3c2b4b.

activist Bree Newsome was hoisted over the fence: Witness the scene at The Tribe CLT, "#KeepItDown Confederate Flag Takedown," June 27, 2015, www.youtube.com/watch?v=gr-mt1P94cQ.

64   *In a move of political expediency*: Eugene Scott, "Nikki Haley: Confed-
     erate Flag 'Should Have Never Been There,'" CNN Politics, July 10,
     2015, www.cnn.com/2015/07/10/politics/nikki-haley-confederate-
     flag-removal.

     nine African Americans in Emanuel AME Church: Let us remember the
     names and families of the deceased: Cynthia Hurd, Susie Jackson,
     Ethel Lee Lance, DePayne Middleton-Doctor, US Senator and Rev-
     erend Clementa Pinckney, Tywanza Sanders, Daniel L. Simmons Sr.,
     Sharonda Coleman-Singleton, and Myra Thompson.

     This massacre left me shocked: Portions of this section were adapted from
     my article "Too Close to Home: Why Charleston Matters to All of Us,"
     CT Pastors, June 2016, www.christianitytoday.com/pastors/2016/june
     -web-exclusives/too-close-to-home.html.

65   *This term refers to the often painful*: Brenda Salter McNeil, *Roadmap to
     Reconciliation: Moving Communities into Unity, Wholeness and Justice*
     (Downers Grove, IL: InterVarsity Press, 2015), 42.

66   *all things are present to God*: Stanley J. Grenz, David Guretzki, and
     Cherith Fee Nordling, *Pocket Dictionary of Theological Terms* (Downers
     Grove, IL: InterVarsity Press, 1999), 86.

67   *God is also omnipotent*: Grenz, Guretzki, and Nordling, *Pocket Dictionary
     of Theological Terms*, 85-86.

6 DELIVERANCE

72   *Thomas Jefferson and Sally Hemmings*: See "Thomas Jefferson and Sally
     Hemings: A Brief Account," Monticello.org, www.monticello.org
     /site/plantation-and-slavery/thomas-jefferson-and-sally-hemings
     -brief-account.

     a society wherein race matters profoundly: Michael O. Emerson and
     Christian Smith, *Divided by Faith: Evangelical Religion and the Problem
     of Race in America* (Oxford: Oxford University Press, 2000), 7.

73   *the way to right wrongs*: Quoted in Patricia A. Schechter, *Ida B. Wells-
     Barnett and American Reform, 1880–1930* (Chapel Hill: The University
     of North Carolina Press, 2001), 89.

     without these moral checks, we re-create: Emerson and Smith, *Divided
     by Faith*, 1.

     a crosscultural continuum: Mark DeYmaz and Oneya Fennell Okuwobi,
     The Multi-Ethnic Christian Life Primer (Little Rock, AR: Mosaix
     Global Network, 2013), 21.

74   *Our tendency to ignore*: Soong-Chan Rah, *Prophetic Lament: A Call for Justice in Troubled Times* (Downers Grove, IL: InterVarsity Press, 2015), 207.

75   *the social construct of race*: For more information about the idea of race, see Alan H. Goodman, Yolanda T. Moses, and Joseph L. Jones, *Race: Are We So Different?* (Malden, MA: Wiley-Blackwell, 2012).

      their forty acres and a mule: See Henry Louis Gates Jr., "The Truth Behind '40 Acres and a Mule,'" The Root, January 7, 2013, www.the root.com/the-truth-behind-40-acres-and-a-mule-1790894780.

77   *changing racial demographics that will soon lead*: Thomas Penny, "U.S. White Population Will Be Minority by 2042, Government Says," Bloomberg, August 14, 2008, www.bloomberg.com/apps/news?pid=n ewsarchive&sid=afLRFXgzpFoY.

79   *Approximately one year later, events*: Portions of this section are adapted from Natasha Sistrunk Robinson, "Race Matters: Last Week & #Ferguson," *A Sista's Journey* (blog), August 22, 2014, https://asistasjourney. com/2014/08/22/race-matters-last-week-ferguson/.

80   *black codes*: Black codes were imposed after the Civil War during President Andrew Johnson's Reconstruction to restrict the work and activity of freed African Americans, mostly in Southern states. A&E Television Networks, "Black Codes," History.com, 2010, www.history .com/topics/black-history/black-codes.

      war on drugs: See Black Media TV, "Jay Z: 'The War on Drugs Is an Epic Fail,'" YouTube, September 15, 2016, www.youtube.com/watch?v =RCWw9DNAUe0. This war on drugs has led to mass incarceration.

      mass incarceration: I highly recommend the Netflix original documentary *13th*, by Ava DuVernay. The trailer can be viewed at www .youtube.com/watch?v=V66F3WU2CKk.

82   *majority of white Americans do not*: Daniel Cox, Juhem Navarro-Rivera, and Robert P. Jones, "Race, Religion, and Political Affiliation of Americans' Core Social Networks," Public Religion Research Institute, August 3, 2016, www.prri.org/research/poll-race-religion-politics -americans-social-networks; Christopher Ingraham, "Three Quarters of Whites Don't Have Any Non-white Friends," *Washington Post*, August, 25, 2014, www.washingtonpost.com/news/wonk/wp/2014 /08/25/three-quarters-of-whites-dont-have-any-non-white-friends /?utm_term=.245ad5da93ca.

82   *lack intimate relationships with nonwhite people*: Emily Swanson, "Do Most White Americans Really Only Have White Friends? Let's Take a Closer Look," HuffPost, September 3, 2014, www.huffingtonpost .com/2014/09/03/black-white-friends-poll_n_5759464.html.

83   *Black Lives Matter Movement*: See "Platform and Demands," Movement for Black Lives, https://policy.m4bl.org/ (accessed November 9, 2016).

      We've got to have some changes: Fannie Lou Hamer, quoted in Donna Ladd, "Fannie Lou Hamer," *Jackson Free Press*, April 15, 2011, www .jacksonfreepress.com/news/2011/apr/15/fannie-lou-hamer.

7 TRUST

89   *being invited, mentored, and sponsored*: For more about these terms, see Natasha Sistrunk Robinson, "The Power of Mentors and Sponsors," *A Sista's Journey* (blog), September 19, 2016, https://asistasjourney. com/2016/09/19/the-power-of-mentors-and-sponsors/.

92   *For the first time he sought*: W. E. B. Du Bois, *The Souls of Black Folk* (New York: Penguin, 1995), 49-50.

      The median wealth of white households: Kristen Bialik, "5 Facts About Blacks in the U.S.," Pew Research Center, February 22, 2018, www.pew research.org/fact-tank/2018/02/22/5-facts-about-blacks-in-the-u-s.

      among full- and part-time workers: Eileen Patten, "Racial, Gender Wage Gaps Persist in U.S. Despite Some Progress," Pew Research Center, July 1, 2016, www.pewresearch.org/fact-tank/2016/07/01 /racial-gender-wage-gaps-persist-in-u-s-despite-some-progress.

      black boys, even ones raised in wealthy families: Adedamola Agboola, "Study: Even When Born into Wealth, Many Black Boys Destined to Become Poor," Black Enterprise, March 29, 2018, www.blackenter prise.com/black-boys-are-destined-to-grow-up-poor-a-new -extensive-study-finds.

      Because of the historical context: Ta-Nehisi Coates, "The Case for Reparations," *Atlantic*, June 2014, www.theatlantic.com/magazine/archive /2014/06/the-case-for-reparations/361631.

93   *Negro poverty is not white poverty*: Lyndon B. Johnson, "Commencement Address at Howard University: 'To Fulfill These Rights,'" June 4, 1965, available at the American Presidency Project, www.presidency.ucsb .edu/ws/?pid=27021; quoted in Coates, "Case for Reparations."

      The wealth gap merely puts: Coates, "Case for Reparations."

96   *Devastated, I quit my job at DHS*: More of this story is told at Natasha Sistrunk Robinson, "I Quit My Job . . . and I'm Not Crazy!," *A Sista's Journey* (blog), April 7, 2011, https://asistasjourney.com/2011/04/07 /coffee-talk-i-quit-my-job-and-im-not-crazy.

98   *The Egyptian magicians repeatedly tried to copy*: See Exodus 7:8-12, 17-24; 8:6-7, 17-18; 9:10-11; 10:1-2; 12:12; 14:4, 18; 16:12.

PART THREE: WILDERNESS

101 *Where is our hope even in*: Soong-Chan Rah, *Prophetic Lament: A Call for Justice in Troubled Times* (Downers Grove, IL: InterVarsity Press, 2015), 29.

8 ANGER

107 *Great leaders often have*: Hitendra Wadhwa, "The Wrath of a Great Leader," *Inc.*, updated January 21, 2013, www.inc.com/hitendra-wadhwa/great -leadership-how-martin-luther-king-jr-wrestled-with-anger.html.

108 *civil rights activist Rev. Dr. C. T. Vivian*: Look up the C. T. Vivian Leadership Institute to find out more; http://ctvli.org/ctvivian.php.

109 *The Romans deliberately used crucifixion*: Richard A. Horsley, *Jesus and Empire: The Kingdom of God and the New World Disorder* (Minneapolis: Fortress, 2003), 28.

     the death of Freddie Gray: See BBC News, "Freddie Gray's Death in Police Custody—What We Know," May 23, 2016, www.bbc.com/news /world-us-canada-32400497.

     Do blacks or the most marginalized: Jamye Wooten, "Who Has the Right to Be Violent?," The BTS Center, November 12, 2015, www .thebtscenter.org/who-has-the-right-to-be-violent.

     Violence is a reaction of whites: John M. Perkins, *Let Justice Roll Down* (Ventura, CA: Regal Books, 1976), 106.

110 *people tend to resort to acts of terrorism*: Horsley, *Jesus and Empire*, 42-43.

     America was founded on violence: Wooten, "Who Has the Right to Be Violent?"

111 *If God stays true*: Soong-Chan Rah, *Prophetic Lament: A Call for Justice in Troubled Times* (Downers Grove, IL: InterVarsity Press, 2015), 76.

9 DEATH

116 *nearly a million people*: Gary A. Haugen and Victor Boutros, *The Locust Effect: Why the End of Poverty Requires the End of Violence* (Oxford: Oxford University Press, 2014), ix.

116   *in a small church compound*: Haugen and Boutros, *Locust Effect*, ix-x.

       What was so clear to me: Haugen and Boutros, *Locust Effect*, x.

118   *Owning our stories*: Brené Brown, "Own Our History. Change the
       Story," Brené Brown (personal website), June 18, 2015, http://brene
       brown.com/blog/2015/06/18/own-our-history-change-the-story.

119   *the gacaca courts*: Thomas Hauschildt, "Gacaca Courts and Restorative
       Justice in Rwanda," E-International Relations, July 15, 2012, www.e-ir
       .info/2012/07/15/gacaca-courts-and-restorative-justice-in-rwanda.

10 HUMILITY

126   *[Leaders and idealists] have a desire*: Simon P. Walker, *Leading Out of
       Who You Are: Discovering the Secret of Undefended Leadership* (Carlisle,
       UK: Piquant, 2007), 16-17.

130   *Pride and despair are twin brothers*: Peter Kreeft, *Back to Virtue: Tradi-
       tional Moral Wisdom for Modern Moral Confusion* (San Francisco: Ig-
       natius, 1992), 103.

132   *each of us is more than*: Bryan Stevenson, *Just Mercy: A Story of Justice
       and Redemption* (New York: Spiegel & Grau, 2014), 17-18.

133   *is a kind of death*: Kreeft, *Back to Virtue*, 107.

134   *would come to find his greatest sense*: Reggie McNeal, *A Work of Heart:
       Understanding How God Shapes Spiritual Leaders* (San Francisco:
       Jossey-Bass, 2011), 13.

11 WAR

138   *This method has a way of disarming*: Martin Luther King Jr., "Address
       at the Freedom Rally in Cobo Hall," in *A Call to Conscience: The
       Landmark Speeches of Dr. Martin Luther King, Jr.*, ed. Clayborne
       Carson and Kris Shepard (New York: Warner Books, 2001), 66-67.

       When Christ calls a man: Dietrich Bonhoeffer, *The Cost of Discipleship*
       (New York: Touchstone, 1959), 89.

       The true power of those lynchings: Bryan Stevenson, *Just Mercy: A Story
       of Justice and Redemption* (New York: Spiegel & Grau, 2014), 30.

139   *the government launched the war on drugs*: To chart this history, I rec-
       ommend rapper Jay Z's short video "The War on Drugs Is an Epic
       Fail," published by Black Media TV, YouTube, September 15, 2016,
       www.youtube.com/watch?v=RCWw9DNAUe0.

139   *This war has helped to create*: I highly recommend Christian rapper Lecrae's TEDx Nashville talk "Heroes and Villains: Is Hip-Hop a Cancer or a Cure?," YouTube, published May 17, 2016, www.youtube .com/watch?v=BFas9cd8ZZ8&t=30s.

The extreme overrepresentation: Stevenson, *Just Mercy*, 301.

Stevenson concludes that the legal institutions: Stevenson, *Just Mercy*, 299-301.

142   *warfare is not simply a matter of force*: Sun Tzu, *The Art of War*, trans. Samuel B. Griffith (London: Oxford University Press, 1963), 41, 66-67, 77.

12 LIVE

Portions of this chapter were adapted from Natasha Sistrunk Robinson, "Ashes to Ashes, Birth to Freedom and Liberation Songs," Missio Alliance, April 28, 2016, www.missioalliance.org/ashes-ashes -birth-freedom-liberation-songs/.

152   *Freedom! Freedom! I can't move*: "Freedom," featuring Kendrick Lamar, track 10 on Beyoncé, *Lemonade*, Parkwood Entertainment/Columbia, 2016.

ballerina Michaela DePrince: Michaela DePrince, "About," www.mich aeladeprince.com/about-1.

153   *Freedom isn't free, but I still*: "Freedom," featuring N'Dambi, track 1 on *Lecrae*, Church Clothes 3, Reach Records, 2016.

I'll rise up: "Rise Up," track 11 on Andra Day, *Cheers to the Fall*, Warner Bros./Buskin, 2015.

Blacks found hope in the music: James H. Cone, *The Cross and the Lynching Tree* (New York: Orbis, 2011), 13.

155   *The most significant 'food'*: Timothy S. Laniak, *Shepherds After My Own Heart: Pastoral Traditions and Leadership in the Bible* (Downers Grove, IL: InterVarsity Press, 2006), 83.

Only as the Israelites obey: Craig G. Bartholomew and Michael W. Goheen, *The Drama of Scripture: Finding Our Place in the Biblical Story* (Grand Rapids: Baker Academic, 2004), 68.

156   *The Reformers said that whenever*: Klaus Bockmuehl, *The Christian Way of Living: An Ethics of the Ten Commandments* (Vancouver, BC: Regent College Publishing, 1994), 22.

159   *What is the world like*: Toni Morrison, quoted in Susan Kelley, "Morrison Speaks on Evil, Language and 'The White Gaze,'" *Cornell Chronicle*, March 11, 2013, http://news.cornell.edu/stories/2013/03/morrison-speaks-evil-language-and-white-gaze.

      In earlier reflections: James H. Cone, *The Cross and the Lynching Tree* (Maryknoll, NY: Orbis, 2011), xvii-xviii, emphasis added.

161   *six principles*: adapted from James W. Sire, *Discipleship of the Mind: Learning to Love God in the Ways We Think* (Downers Grove, IL: InterVarsity Press, 1990), 136-38.

      The Word gives life: See 1 Samuel 2:6; Psalm 36:9; Nehemiah 9:6; Acts 17:25; 1 Timothy 6:13.

13 BUILD

168   *Sponsors, on the other hand*: For more on this topic, see Natasha Sistrunk Robinson, "The Power of Mentors and Sponsors," *A Sista's Journey* (blog), September 19, 2016, https://asistasjourney.com/2016/09/19/the-power-of-mentors-and-sponsors.

169   *They recruit people of color*: Helen Kim Ho, "8 Ways People of Color are Tokenized in Nonprofits," The Nonprofit Revolution, September 18, 2017, https://medium.com/the-nonprofit-revolution/8-ways-people-of-color-are-tokenized-in-nonprofits-32138d0860c1.

170   *the bias in judgment and/or behavior*: National Center for State Courts, "Helping Courts Address Implicit Bias," www.ncsc.org/ibreport (accessed May 16, 2017). The NCSC has removed these resources from their website with plans to update them by late 2018 (see www.ncsc.org/ibeducation).

      We all want progress: C. S. Lewis, *Mere Christianity* (New York: HarperCollins, 1980), 28.

172   *intersectionality*: Kimberlé Chenshaw, "The Urgency of Intersectionality," TED, October 2016, www.ted.com/talks/kimberle_crenshaw_the_urgency_of_intersectionality; or her article "Demarginalizing the Intersection of Race and Sex: A Black Feminist Critique of Antidiscrimination Doctrine, Feminist Theory and Antiracist Politics," *University of Chicago Legal Forum* 1989, no. 1 (1989), https://chicagounbound.uchicago.edu/uclf/vol1989/iss1/8.

172 *They fought against injustices*: Portions of this section are adapted from Natasha Sistrunk Robinson, "'Hidden Figures' Teaches How Injustice Remains Hidden," Missio Alliance, January 12, 2017, www.missioalliance.org/hidden-figures-teaches-injustice-remains-hidden.

Whatever Dorothy learned, she taught: "When you learn, teach. When you get, give" is a treasured lesson taught by Dr. Maya Angelou. See Natasha Sistrunk Robinson, "When You Learn, Teach," *SheLoves Magazine*, August 20, 2014, http://shelovesmagazine.com/2014/learn-teach.

I've been mentored by dead people: See "I'm Being Mentored by a Dead Guy," "Mentoring Resources . . . Finally," and "Leadership: What About Your Friends?" at *A Sista's Journey* (blog), www.asistasjourney.com; "Are You My Mentor?," *CT Pastors*, December 2013, www.christianitytoday.com/pastors/2013/december-online-only/are-you-my-mentor.html.

174 *actively take part in*: Leadership LINKS Creed. Check out www.leadershiplinksinc.org.

175 *being mentored by people of color*: See Natasha Sistrunk Robinson, "Mentoring Across the Lines," *Today's Christian Woman*, February 2014, www.todayschristianwoman.com/articles/2014/february/mentoring-across-lines.html.

The task of future Christian leaders: Henri Nouwen, In the Name of Jesus: Reflections on Christian Leadership (New York: Crossroad, 1989), 87-88.

176 *the right people, in the right place*: Leadership LINKS Creed.

177 *Right now, you have the choice*: Check out my book *Mentor for Life: Finding Purpose Through Intentional Discipleship* and its accompanying Leader's Training resource to prepare for the important kingdom work of mentoring individuals and small groups.

14 HEAL

182 *Images and conversations depicting*: Bree Newsome, "Charlottesville Reinforced That Self-Care Is an Essential Part of My Activism," Self, August 17, 2017, www.self.com/story/charlottesville-activism-self-care.

Self-care gives us all a joyful resistance: Good old-fashioned humor, healthy relationships, and sleep can decrease stress and help the heart. See American Heart Association, "Humor Helps Your Heart? How?,"

April 5, 2017, www.heart.org/HEARTORG/HealthyLiving/Humor
-helps-your-heart-How_UCM_447039_Article.jsp#.Wk0iO9
-nHcs; Harvard Heart Letter, "A Good Night's Sleep: Advice to Take
to Heart," Harvard Health Publishing, September 2017, www.health
.harvard.edu/heart-health/a-good-nights-sleep-advice-to-take-to
-heart; Harvard Women's Health Watch, "Stress and Your Heart,"
Harvard Health Publishing, December 2013, www.health.harvard
.edu/heart-health/stress-and-your-heart; Johns Hopkins Medicine,
"Are Your Relationships Putting Your Heart at Risk?," www.hopkins
medicine.org/health/healthy_heart/know_your_risks/are-your
-relationships-putting-your-heart-at-risk; Debra Umberson and
Jennifer Karas Montez, "Social Relationships and Health: A Flash-
point for Health Policy," *Journal of Health and Social Behavior* 51, no.
S1 (2010): S54-66, www.ncbi.nlm.nih.gov/pmc/articles/PMC3150158.

183   *false narratives about evangelicalism*: See Natasha Sistrunk Robinson,
      "Being Black, a Woman and an Evangelical," Missio Alliance, May
      23, 2017, www.missioalliance.org/black-woman-evangelical/.

184   *My most meaningful calling*: Ann Voskamp, *The Broken Way: A Daring
      Path into the Abundant Life* (Grand Rapids: Zondervan, 2016), 221.

      We can be brokers of healing: Voskamp, *Broken Way*, 221.

      laying down [our lives] means: Henri Nouwen, *In the Name of Jesus:
      Reflections on Christian Leadership* (New York: Crossroad, 1989), 61.

185   *a peacemaker and not a "peace faker"*: Sande describes three ways people
      respond to conflict: (1) escaping or faking peace, (2) attacking or
      breaking peace, and (3) making peace. Ken Sande, *The Peacemaker: A
      Biblical Guide to Resolving Personal Conflict*, rev. ed. (Grand Rapids:
      Baker Books, 2004), 22.

      We are not the healers: Nouwen, *In the Name of Jesus*, 61-62.

186   *The Greek language includes four words*: Natasha Sistrunk Robinson,
      Mentor for Life: Finding Purpose Through Intentional Discipleship
      (Grand Rapids: Zondervan, 2016), 171.

      The gospel shows us: Sande, *Peacemaker*, 117.

187   *forgiveness can be delayed when*: Sande, *Peacemaker*, 133.

      consequences of restitution or reparations: Read about God's instructions
      to the Israelites regarding restitution for wrongs in Numbers 5:5-10.

188   *learning to forgive*: Reggie McNeal, *A Work of Heart: Understanding How
      God Shapes Spiritual Leaders* (San Francisco: Jossey-Bass, 2011), 126.

188   *a church where we were ethnic minorities*: I first wrote about our experience in my blog post "Hot Topic: I Go to Church with White People," *A Sista's Journey* (blog), March 25, 2011, https://asistasjourney .com/2011/03/25/hot-topic-i-go-to-church-with-white-people.

189   *That is why I teach*: Patricia Raybon, *My First White Friend: Confessions on Race, Love, and Forgiveness* (New York: Penguin, 1996), 208.

190   *Spiritual leaders who quit loving*: McNeal, *Work of Heart*, 126.

15 LIGHT

195   *Brother Martin delivered this famous speech*: Clayborne Carson and Kris Shepard, eds., *A Call to Conscience: The Landmark Speeches of Dr. Martin Luther King, Jr.* (New York: Warner Books, 2001), 201.

   often discussed this near-death experience: Carson and Shepard, *Call to Conscience*, 202.

   If something isn't done: Martin Luther King Jr., "I've Been to the Mountaintop" (1968), in Carson and Shepard, *Call to Conscience*, 210.

196   *If I were standing at the beginning*: King, in *Call to Conscience*, 209.

197   *Whenever Pharaoh wanted*: King, in *Call to Conscience*, 210.

   Be concerned about your brother: King, in *Call to Conscience*, 217.

200   *I just want to do God's will*: King, in *Call to Conscience*, 222-23.

201   *For the pious person*: Abraham Heschel, quoted in Joseph Harp Britton, *Abraham Heschel and the Phenomenon of Piety* (New York: Bloomsbury, 2013), 144.

16 HOME

206   *transformed people needed to cease imitating*: Donald T. Phillips, *Martin Luther King, Jr. on Leadership: Inspiration & Wisdom for Challenging Times* (New York: Warner Books, 1999), 127, 130-31.

209   *tend to choose slow death*: Robert E. Quinn, *Building the Bridge as You Walk on It: A Guide for Leading Change* (San Francisco: Jossey-Bass, 2004), 19.

ABOUT THE AUTHOR

 **Natasha Sistrunk Robinson** is the visionary founder and chairperson of Leadership LINKS, Inc. She is the author of *Mentor for Life: Finding Purpose Through Intentional Discipleship*, *Mentor for Life Leader's Training Manual*, and the Bible study *Hope for Us: Knowing God Through the Nicene Creed*. Natasha is a graduate of the US Naval Academy (BS, English) and Gordon-Conwell Theological Seminary Charlotte (MA, Christian Leadership). A regular columnist for *Outreach* magazine, writer at *Missio Alliance*, and blogger at *A Sista's Journey*, she has also written more than one hundred articles for publications such as *Christianity Today* and Urban Ministries, Inc. (including *Urban Faith* magazine).

A former Marine Corps officer, Natasha has nearly twenty years of leadership and mentoring experience in diverse settings, including the military, federal government, church, seminary, and nonprofit sectors. Natasha uses her advocacy work for anti–human trafficking efforts and to pursue equity for women and the impoverished. She is a sought-after international speaker, Bible teacher, leadership consultant, and mentoring coach. Natasha is encouraged to live her truth through her village of family and friends, including her daughter, Ashley, and husband, Deronta.

Use #ASojournersTruth to join the conversation!

FOLLOW NATASHA SISTRUNK ROBINSON

- Official website: NatashaSRobinson.com
- Blog: asistasjourney.com
- Facebook.com/NatashaSistrunkRobinson
- Instagram: asistasjourney
- Twitter: asistasjourney

NSR NATASHA SISTRUNK ROBINSON

◠ LEADERSHIPLINKS

Leadership LINKS, Inc. is a growing 501(c)(3) faith-based, educational organization. Founded by U.S. Naval Academy alumni, we use our core values of Love, Inspiration, Network, Knowledge, and Service to enrich communities through leadership, mentoring, and education.

We exist to educate and equip servant leaders who are committed to using their skills and resources for the greater good of humanity.

Our vision is to connect people with purpose.

Our mission is to offer leadership education that facilitates impactful living, character and spiritual development.

Leadership LINKS intentionally connects with students from ethnically and economically diverse backgrounds. We use our resources and programming to encourage these young people toward innovation, entrepreneurship, and executive leadership. We are building a collaborative network to ensure that our LINKS Leaders receive access and opportunities to live their lives on purpose through personal and professional development, which allows for impactful living that glorifies God while working in our homes, classrooms, communities, and philanthropic efforts in the ministry, marketplace, or throughout the world.

LINK UP WITH US

Learn about our leadership education resources and programming and how to get involved.

Email: admin@leadershiplinksinc.org
Web: www.leadershiplinksinc.org
Facebook: LeadershipLINKSInc
Twitter: LINKSLead
Instagram: leadershiplinks

Note: The views expressed throughout this book are the author's own and do not represent the views of the organization.

ance

and

≈ INTERVARSITY PRESS

Missio Alliance has arisen in response to the shared voice of pastors and ministry leaders from across the landscape of North American Christianity for a new "space" of togetherness and reflection amid the issues and challenges facing the church in our day. We are united by a desire for a fresh expression of evangelical faith, one significantly informed by the global evangelical family. Lausanne's Cape Town Commitment, "A Confession of Faith and a Call to Action," provides an excellent guidepost for our ethos and aims.

In partnership with InterVarsity Press, we are pleased to offer a line of resources authored by a diverse range of theological practitioners. The resources in this series are selected based on the important way in which they address and embody these values, and thus, the unique contribution they offer in equipping Christian leaders for fuller and more faithful participation in God's mission.

Available Titles

The Church as Movement by JR Woodward and Dan White Jr., 978-0-8308-4133-2

Emboldened by Tara Beth Leach, 978-0-8308-4524-8

Embrace by Leroy Barber, 978-0-8308-4471-5

Faithful Presence by David E. Fitch, 978-0-8308-4127-1

God Is Stranger by Krish Kandiah, 978-0-8308-4532-3

Paradoxology by Krish Kandiah, 978-0-8308-4504-0

Redeeming Sex by Debra Hirsch, 978-0-8308-3639-0

Seven Practices for the Church on Mission by David E. Fitch, 978-0-8308-4142-4

White Awake by Daniel Hill, 978-0-8308-4393-0

missioalliance.org | twitter.com/missioalliance | facebook.com/missioalliance